AAT

Synoptic Assessment
Level 2
Foundation Certificate in Accounting
Question Bank

Fourth edition 2018

ISBN 9781 5097 1886 3

British Library Cataloguing-in-Publication Data
A catalogue record for this book is available
from the British Library

Published by

BPP Learning Media Ltd
BPP House, Aldine Place
142-144 Uxbridge Road
London W12 8AA

www.bpp.com/learningmedia

Printed in the United Kingdom

Your learning materials, published by
BPP Learning Media Ltd, are printed on
paper obtained from traceable
sustainable sources.

The contents of this course material are intended
as a guide and not professional advice.
Although every effort has been made to ensure
that the contents of this course material are
correct at the time of going to press, BPP
Learning Media makes no warranty that the
information in this course material is accurate or
complete and accept no liability for any loss or
damage suffered by any person acting or
refraining from acting as a result of the material
in this course material.

We are grateful to the AAT for permission to
reproduce the sample assessment(s). The
answers to the sample assessment(s) have been
published by the AAT. All other answers have
been prepared by BPP Learning Media Ltd.

A note about copyright

Dear Customer

What does the little © mean and why does it matter?

Your market-leading BPP books, course materials and e-
learning materials do not write and update themselves.
People write them on their own behalf or as employees of
an organisation that invests in this activity. Copyright law
protects their livelihoods. It does so by creating rights
over the use of the content.

Breach of copyright is a form of theft – as well as being a
criminal offence in some jurisdictions, it is potentially a
serious breach of professional ethics.

With current technology, things might seem a bit hazy
but, basically, without the express permission of BPP
Learning Media:

- Photocopying our materials is a breach of
  copyright

- Scanning, ripcasting or conversion of our digital
  materials into different file formats, uploading them
  to Facebook or e-mailing them to your friends is a
  breach of copyright

You can, of course, sell your books, in the form in which
you have bought them – once you have finished with
them. (Is this fair to your fellow students? We update for a
reason.) Please note the e-products are sold on a single
user licence basis: we do not supply 'unlock' codes to
people who have bought them secondhand.

And what about outside the UK? BPP Learning Media
strives to make our materials available at prices students
can afford by local printing arrangements, pricing
policies and partnerships which are clearly listed on our
website. A tiny minority ignore this and indulge in
criminal activity by illegally photocopying our material or
supporting organisations that do. If they act illegally and
unethically in one area, can you really trust them?

BPP
LEARNING MEDIA

Contents

Introduction

This is BPP Learning Media's AAT Question Bank for the *Foundation Certificate in Accounting Level 2 Synoptic Assessment*. It is part of a suite of ground-breaking resources produced by BPP Learning Media for AAT assessments.

This Question Bank has been carefully designed to enable students to practise all of the learning outcomes and assessment criteria for the units that make up the *Foundation Certificate in Accounting Level 2 Synoptic Assessment*. It is fully up to date as at June 2018 and reflects both the AAT's qualification specification and the sample assessment provided by the AAT.

This Question Bank contains these key features:

- Tasks corresponding to each assessment objective in the qualification specification and related task in the synoptic assessment. Some tasks in this Question Bank are designed for learning purposes, others are of assessment standard.

- AAT's AQ2016 sample assessment and answers for the *Foundation Certificate in Accounting Level 2 Synoptic Assessment* and further BPP practice assessments

The emphasis in all tasks and assessments is on the practical application of the skills acquired.

VAT

You may find tasks throughout this Question Bank that need you to calculate or be aware of a rate of VAT. This is stated at 20% in these examples and questions.

Test specification

Assessment method	Marking type	Duration of assessment
Computer based synoptic assessment	Partially computer/partially human marked	2 hours

Synoptic assessment objectives		Weighting
Assessment objective 1 Related learning outcomes:	**Demonstrate an understanding of the finance function and the roles and procedures carried out by members of an accounting team** Working Effectively in Finance LO1 Understand the finance function within an organisation LO2 Use personal skills development in finance LO3 Produce work effectively LO4 Understand corporate social responsibility (CSR), ethics and sustainability within organisations	24%
Assessment objective 2 Related learning outcomes:	**Process transactions, complete calculations and make journal entries** Bookkeeping Transactions LO2 Process customer transactions LO3 Process supplier transactions LO4 Process receipts and payments LO5 Process transactions through the ledgers to the trial balance	24%
Assessment objective 3 Related learning outcomes:	**Compare, produce and reconcile journals and accounts** Bookkeeping Controls LO3 Use control accounts LO4 Use the journal LO5 Reconcile a bank statement with the cash book Elements of costing LO2 Use cost recording techniques LO3 Provide information on actual and budgeted costs and income	34%
Assessment objective 4 Related learning outcomes:	**Communicate financial information effectively** Work Effectively in Finance LO3 Produce work effectively	18%
Total		**100%**

Approaching the assessment

When you sit the assessment it is very important that you follow the on screen instructions. This means you need to carefully read the instructions, both on the introduction screens and during specific tasks.

When you access the assessment you should be presented with an introductory screen with information similar to that shown below (taken from the introductory screen from one of the AAT's AQ2016 sample assessments for the *Foundation Certificate in Accounting Level 2 Synoptic Assessment*).

We have provided the following **sample assessment** to help you familiarise yourself with AAT's e-assessment environment.
It is designed to demonstrate as many as possible of the question types you may find in a live assessment.
It is not designed to be used on its own to determine whether you are ready for a live assessment.

At the end of this sample assessment you will receive an immediate result. This will **not** take into account your response to Task 6.
In the live assessment this task will be human marked, so you will not receive an immediate result.

Assessment information

Instructions

- Read the scenario carefully before attempting the questions, you can return to it at any time by clicking on the 'Introduction' button at the bottom of the screen.
- Complete all 7 tasks.
- Answer the questions in the spaces provided. For answers requiring free text entry, the box will expand to fit your answer.
- Task 6 requires extended writing as part of your response to the question. You should make sure you allow adequate time to complete this task.
- You must use a full stop to indicate a decimal point. For example, write 100.57 **not** 100,57 or 100 57
- Both minus signs and brackets can be used to indicate negative numbers **unless** task instructions say otherwise.
- You may use a comma to indicate a number in the thousands, but you don't have to. For example, 10000 and 10,000 are both acceptable.
- Where the date is relevant, it is given in the task data.

Information

- The total time for this paper is 2 hours.
- The total mark for this paper is 100.
- The marks for each sub-task are shown alongside the task.

The actual instructions will vary depending on the subject you are studying for. It is very important you read the instructions on the introductory screen and apply them in the assessment. You don't want to lose marks when you know the correct answer just because you have not entered it in the right format.

In general, the rules set out in the AAT sample assessments for the subject you are studying for will apply in the real assessment, but you should carefully read the information on this screen again in the real assessment, just to make sure. This screen may also confirm the VAT rate used if applicable.

A full stop is needed to indicate a decimal point. We would recommend using minus signs to indicate negative numbers and leaving out the comma signs to indicate thousands, as this results in a lower number of key strokes and less margin for error when working under time pressure. Having said that, you can use

whatever is easiest for you as long as you operate within the rules set out for your particular assessment.

You have to show competence throughout the assessment and you should therefore complete all of the tasks. Don't leave questions unanswered.

In some assessments, written or complex tasks may be human marked. In this case you are given a blank space or table to enter your answer into. You are told in the assessments which tasks these are. **Note.** There may be none if all answers are marked by the computer.

If these involve calculations, it is a good idea to decide in advance how you are going to lay out your answers to such tasks by practising answering them on a word document, and certainly you should try all such tasks in this Question Bank and in the AAT's environment using the sample assessment.

When asked to fill in tables, or gaps, never leave any blank even if you are unsure of the answer. Fill in your best estimate.

Note that for some assessments where there is a lot of scenario information or tables of data provided (eg tax tables), you may need to access these via 'pop-ups'. Instructions will be provided on how you can bring up the necessary data during the assessment.

Finally, take note of any task specific instructions once you are in the assessment. For example you may be asked to enter a date in a certain format or to enter a number to a certain number of decimal places.

Grading

To achieve the qualification and to be awarded a grade, you must pass all the mandatory unit assessments, all optional unit assessments (where applicable) and the synoptic assessment.

The AAT Level 2 Foundation Certificate in Accounting will be awarded a grade. This grade will be based on performance across the qualification. Unit assessments and synoptic assessments are not individually graded. These assessments are given a mark that is used in calculating the overall grade.

How overall grade is determined

You will be awarded an overall qualification grade (Distinction, Merit, and Pass). If you do not achieve the qualification you will not receive a qualification certificate, and the grade will be shown as unclassified.

The marks of each assessment will be converted into a percentage mark and rounded up or down to the nearest whole number. This percentage mark is then weighted according to the weighting of the unit assessment or synoptic assessment within the qualification. The resulting weighted assessment percentages are combined to arrive at a percentage mark for the whole qualification.

Grade definition	Percentage threshold
Distinction	90–100%
Merit	80–89%
Pass	70–79%
Unclassified	0–69% Or failure to pass one or more assessment/s

Re-sits

Some AAT qualifications such as the AAT Foundation Certificate in Accounting have restrictions in place for how many times you are able to re-sit assessments. Please refer to the AAT website for further details.

You should only be entered for an assessment when you are well prepared and you expect to pass the assessment.

AAT qualifications

The material in this book may support the following AAT qualifications:

AAT Foundation Certificate in Accounting Level 2, AAT Foundation Certificate in Accounting at SCQF Level 5 and AAT Foundation Diploma in Accounting and Business Level 2.

Supplements

From time to time we may need to publish supplementary materials to one of our titles. This can be for a variety of reasons. From a small change in the AAT unit guidance to new legislation coming into effect between editions.

You should check our supplements page regularly for anything that may affect your learning materials. All supplements are available free of charge on our supplements page on our website at:

http://www.bpp.com/learning-media/about/students

Improving material and removing errors

There is a constant need to update and enhance our study materials in line with both regulatory changes and new insights into the assessments.

From our team of authors BPP appoints a subject expert to update and improve these materials for each new edition.

Their updated draft is subsequently technically checked by another author and from time to time non-technically checked by a proof reader.

We are very keen to remove as many numerical errors and narrative typos as we can but given the volume of detailed information being changed in a short space of time we know that a few errors will sometimes get through our net.

We apologise in advance for any inconvenience that an error might cause. We continue to look for new ways to improve these study materials and would welcome your suggestions. If you have any comments about this book, please email nisarahmed@bpp.com or write to Nisar Ahmed, AAT Head of Programme, BPP Learning Media Ltd, BPP House, Aldine Place, London W12 8AA.

Question Bank

Assessment objective 1 – Work Effectively in Finance

Task 1

An organisation has five directors. The organisation chart below shows the directors of the organisation and staff working in the finance function.

(a) **Add the correct job titles into the blank spaces to complete this part of the organisation chart.**

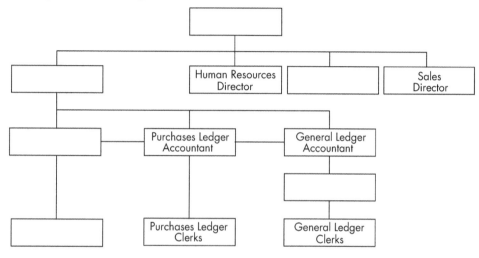

Job roles:

Assistant General Ledger Accountant	Human Resources Manager	Production Supervisor	Auditor	Production Director	IT Consultant
Tax Inspector	Estates Assistant	Finance Director	Sales Ledger Accountant	Managing Director	Sales Ledger Clerks

(b) Identify which TWO of the following actions will help the solvency of an organisation:

Action	✓
Maximise inventory levels	
Issue statements to trade receivables on a regular basis	
Pay trade payables as soon as invoices are received	
Encourage trade receivables to pay the amounts owed on or before the due date	
Ensure the organisation has a staff development policy	
Issue statements to trade payables on a regular basis	

Task 2

You have been asked to do an urgent task by your manager which will mean you will not be able to complete the work a senior colleague has already allocated to you to complete by the end of the day.

(a) Select the most appropriate action to take from the list provided in the table.

Action	✓
Complete the additional task as your manager is the most senior person you work for and do whatever other work you can. The colleague will have to wait for their work until you have time to complete it.	
Complete the additional task as your manager is the most senior person you work for and do whatever other work you can. You will prioritise the colleague's work for the next day.	
Complete the colleague's work as they asked you to do the work first and you will start the manager's work tomorrow.	
Discuss your workload with both the manager and the colleague to decide on the work priority and renegotiate deadlines where appropriate.	

You have to check supplier statements on a Thursday so that your colleague can receive the necessary information for her to be able to pay appropriate suppliers. A critically important task has been left on your desk by your manager. If you complete this urgent task you will not be able to check all the supplier statements and provide information to your colleague.

(b) Identify whether the following statements are true or false in relation to the impact on your colleague or the organisation if you do not supply the information on supplier statements:

Statement	True ✓	False ✓
There will be no impact. If you can't check supplier statements on Thursday, you can prioritise this work the next day.		
Your colleague may be unable to pay suppliers by the due date which may result in problems for the organisation in receiving future supplies.		

The area of the accounting function you work in is arranged as a team of four people – a manager and three team members.

(c) Identify which THREE considerations are important to ensuring the team works effectively.

Team effectiveness

Considerations:

All staff have the same skills, knowledge and experience	Each team member is willing and able to cover the work of other team members if necessary
All team members know only their own job role	Team members work solely within their own job role
All team members have clearly defined objectives and responsibilities	Good communication within the team

Task 3

(a) **Identify which FOUR of the following are sustainability initiatives that a business may implement.**

	✓
Arrange virtual rather than face to face team meetings	
Have all office lighting linked to motion sensors so they automatically switch off when the office is empty	
Always select the lowest priced suppliers of goods and services	
Ensure all trainee accountants complete CPD	
Do business only with organisations which can demonstrate they follow responsible environmental practices	
Ensure costs and expenses are minimised in every instance	
Arrange monthly management meetings at a central point in the country rather than at head office	
Restrict paper usage to the printing of essential documents only	

(b) **Identify whether the following statements are true or false:**

Statement	True ✓	False ✓
Sustainability means ensuring the organisation focuses purely on generating the highest profit irrespective of the consequences of the organisation's actions.		
When building new premises, trying to ensure the building is carbon neutral even if this results in increased initial costs is an example of a sustainable initiative by the organisation.		
Sustainable initiatives do not apply to those in an accounting function but such initiatives do apply to the production function.		
Having a policy of office buildings being well insulated and solar powered may help to reduce the running costs of the organisation and also have a positive effect on the environment.		

Task 4

It is important to understand you will be required to follow policies and procedures in the completion of your work. Some policies and procedures will apply solely to those working in a finance function and other policies and procedures will apply to employees across the whole organisation, including those working in the finance function.

(a) **Which ONE of the following policies and procedures is most likely to be relevant to those working in an accounting function?**

	✓
Company vehicle servicing policy	
Sales visit procedures	
Expenses payment procedures	
Production shift handover procedures	

(b) **Identify which TWO of the following statements are correct:**

	✓
The accounting function has a legal obligation to review the credit policy every two years.	
Organisational procedures prevent staff from suggesting improvements to work processes.	
It is good practice for organisations to explain the fire evacuation procedures during staff induction training.	
The Staff Development policy only applies to those working in the human resources department.	
Many organisational policies and procedures are designed to ensure that working practices comply with legal requirements.	
The Data Protection policy is an example of a policy that would not apply to those staff working in an accounting function.	

Task 5

You are a trainee in the accounting function and you work for both the financial accounting and management accounting functions. You work from 9:00am until 1:00pm daily.

The following table shows your work schedule for the financial accounting function which details the days in the month when specific jobs have to be completed and the length of time, in hours, each job takes you to complete. The financial

accounting function works on a monthly cycle of work and the work required for the end of the day is identified in the work schedule.

You also work for Sue Baines, the Management Accountant, but this work allocation is less structured. Sue usually allocates work by leaving you notes explaining the work she needs to be completed, the expected duration of the work and when it has to be completed by.

Financial accounting function work schedule					
	Monday	Tuesday	Wednesday	Thursday	Friday
Week 1	Bank reconciliation (2 hours)			Bank monies (2 hours)	Debtor review (3 hours)
Week 2	Wages analysis (1 hour)	Petty cash top up (1 hour)	Supplier payments (3 hours)	Bank monies (2 hours)	
Week 3	Bank reconciliation (2 hours)			Bank monies (2 hours)	
Week 4	Accruals and prepayments (2 hours)		Fixed assets (1 hour)	Bank monies (2 hours)	Debtor review (3 hours)

Note from Sue
Week 2

Hi,

I have some jobs for you to complete this week. I have a meeting with the Sales Director on Tuesday afternoon and I need an analysis of expenses for Region 6 to take to that meeting. I shall leave the office at 12:00pm on Tuesday. I know that there are some expenses waiting to be processed and I have been advised these will be completed by close of business on Monday so it is important that you do not start the analysis before these expenses are processed. I expect the analysis to take you about two hours.

On Monday I need to complete an exercise on stock analysis and so I need a breakdown of closing stock by month for each of the months in the current financial year. I think this is about a two hour job but I need the information by 11:00am. Could you also complete the usual regional reconciliation by 12:00pm on Monday, this usually takes you an hour.

Thanks,

Sue

In addition to the above information, the whole accounting function has an hour-long meeting at 9:00am on Tuesdays. Today is Monday of week 2 of the month and you are required to identify, using the to-do lists below, what jobs you will do for today and tomorrow and when you will do them.

Complete the to-do list below for Monday and Tuesday of week 2 by assigning each task to the correct position.

Please note that each task box is one hour in duration, therefore if a task takes more than one hour to complete you will be able to use the task box more than once.

Monday To-do list	Tuesday To-do list	Time
		09:00–10:00
		10:00–11:00
		11:00–12:00
		12:00–13:00

Tasks:

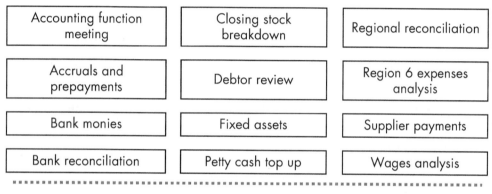

Accounting function meeting	Closing stock breakdown	Regional reconciliation
Accruals and prepayments	Debtor review	Region 6 expenses analysis
Bank monies	Fixed assets	Supplier payments
Bank reconciliation	Petty cash top up	Wages analysis

Task 6

An accounting trainee who is studying for an AAT Level 2 qualification is about to start a new role working in the management accounts function. The priority in the first three months will be for the trainee to take over responsibility for the production and distribution of the monthly budget reports from a colleague. It is critical that this work is addressed without delay as the colleague is moving to another work location very shortly. In the following three-month period, the trainee will then be supporting the assistant management accountant who has been given the task of introducing standard costing methods into the production department.

(a) **Insert the TWO most appropriate development activities that the trainee should undertake in the first six months of taking up the new role in the management accounts function. The order in which you place the activities is important, and you should place the activity with the highest importance first in the table.**

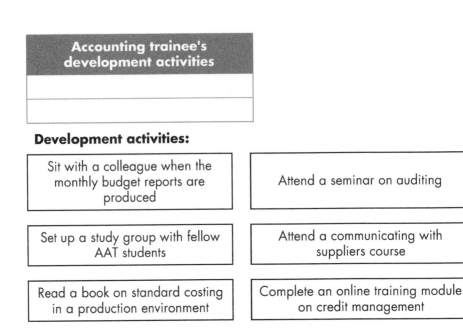

Accounting trainee's development activities

Development activities:

Sit with a colleague when the monthly budget reports are produced	Attend a seminar on auditing
Set up a study group with fellow AAT students	Attend a communicating with suppliers course
Read a book on standard costing in a production environment	Complete an online training module on credit management
Complete a buyer's course	Complete training on the purchases ledger computer system

(b) Identify **TWO** of the following statements which are consequences to the organisation and/or the individual of **NOT** maintaining appropriate and sufficient CPD activities. Insert the appropriate statements into the table provided. The order in which you place the items is not important.

Consequences of NOT maintaining CPD activities

Reasons:

Work performance will improve.	If knowledge is not up to date then staff could give incorrect professional advice.
Development activities will take account of future needs of the job role.	New skills will be acquired and career prospects enhanced.
A chartered accountant may be prevented from continuing as a member of their professional body.	It will be easier to cover colleagues' job roles when they are on holiday.

(c) **Identify whether the following statements are true or false in relation to the completion of CPD activity.**

Statement	True ✓	False ✓
Conducting research in the library at the local college as part of your AAT studies is one type of CPD activity.		
Making sure that an accounting trainee has completed sufficient CPD activities is the sole responsibility of the organisation's Human Resources department.		

Task 7

It is important that those who work within an accounting function uphold fundamental ethical principles.

The table below details four situations which may arise in business.

(a) **From the options provided select the fundamental ethical principle that applies in each situation. Note each option may be used more than once.**

Situation	Fundamental ethical principle applicable
You are asked by a colleague to provide the contact details of a client as they were at school together.	
You have been asked to complete a VAT return which is a subject you have not yet studied at college and about which you have little knowledge.	
Your organisation has a Disciplinary and Grievance policy which applies to all staff in the organisation from the most senior partner down.	
A new accountant asks you to check an advertisement which is to be placed in the local newspaper. In this he states 'We are the best accountants in the area and half the price of Jones and Co'.	

Options:

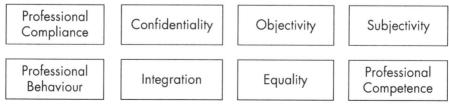

Professional Compliance	Confidentiality	Objectivity	Subjectivity
Professional Behaviour	Integration	Equality	Professional Competence

Conflicts of interest may arise during your work as an accountant and it is important you act correctly when they occur.

(b) Review each of the following situations and select the most appropriate course of action from the options provided.

(i) Whilst conducting a year-end audit at a client's business the client offers to take you on an all-expenses paid holiday to her villa in Spain once you have finished the year-end work.

	✓
Politely decline the offer and do not tell anyone about it.	
Politely accept the offer but ask the client not to mention the holiday to any other members of the audit team.	
Politely accept the offer and work extremely hard to finish the year-end work.	
Politely decline the offer and discuss the situation with your manager.	

(ii) You have been asked to act as an interviewer to help assess and select prospective new trainees for your organisation. Your niece has been selected for one of the interviews.

	✓
Complete the work as interviewer but treat each interviewee fairly and don't tell anyone about your connection with one of the applicants.	
Complete the work as interviewer and ensure you are able to help your niece through to the next stage of the recruitment process.	
Refuse to be involved in any aspect of the assessment and selection of prospective trainees but do not explain to your manager why.	
Discuss the situation with your manager to see if you could complete the work but abstain from being involved in the assessment of your niece.	

(iii) You have been asked by a family friend to advise them of the names of current bidders and details of their offers regarding a contract that they wish to tender for.

	✓
Provide them with the requested details of current bidders and their offers.	
Provide them with the requested details of the names of the bidders but not the details of their offers.	
Politely decline to provide any details explaining you are not allowed to disclose such information.	
Provide them with incorrect details of the other bidders' offers.	

(c) When can information about a client be disclosed to their spouse?

▼

Picklist:

Always, they are spouses so you can disclose information.
Never, in no circumstances can you ever disclose information to a spouse.
Sometimes, but only if you have the permission of the client.

Task 8

You work for a company in the accounts department. You have been passed a company 'information' policy that your manager says is relevant to you when carrying out your daily tasks.

An extract from the policy is given below:

Information policy

- Personal data must be accurate.

- Personal data must only be kept for as long as necessary.

- Personal data must be kept securely.

- No information about customers or employees must be revealed to other customers or employees.

(a) **Complete the following sentence by selecting the appropriate option from the picklist.**

This policy has been compiled to aid compliance with [▼]

Picklist:

Confidentiality of Information Legislation.
Data Protection Legislation.
Employee Protection Legislation.

The accounting department will provide information to other departments within the business.

(b) **Select ONE type of information that will be provided by the accounting department to EACH of the departments shown as follows.**

Draw lines between the left hand side and right hand side boxes to indicate your selections. (CBT instruction: Select your answer by clicking on the left hand box and then on the right hand box. You can remove a line by clicking on it.)

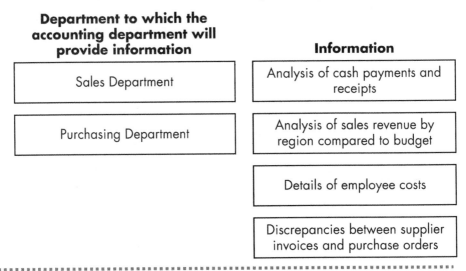

Department to which the accounting department will provide information	Information
Sales Department	Analysis of cash payments and receipts
Purchasing Department	Analysis of sales revenue by region compared to budget
	Details of employee costs
	Discrepancies between supplier invoices and purchase orders

Task 9

For each of the following actions, indicate whether they primarily contribute to:

- Compliance with applicable laws and regulations
- The management of working capital and solvency
- The smooth running of the business

Action	Contributes to:
Reduce customer credit terms so they pay their debts earlier	▼
Ensure IT support is in place in case staff encounter computer problems	▼
Produce a Health and Safety policy to be circulated to all staff	▼
Ensure all staff are paid at least the minimum wage	▼
Ensure staff recruited for each job have the relevant experience and skills	▼
Avoid the build-up of surplus inventories	▼

Picklist:

Compliance with applicable laws and regulations
The management of working capital and solvency
The smooth running of the business

Task 10

(a) **Complete the following sentence.**

A(n) [▼] is used to show the structure of an organisation or function.

Picklist:

job description
organisation chart
person specification
personnel chart

An accounting department, headed up by the finance director (James Smith), also has:

- A financial accountant (Jill Jones)
- A management accountant (Bill Williams)
- A management accounts assistant (Emily Brooks)
- A financial accounts assistant (Nicky Rivers)

(b) **Which TWO of the following statements are true?**

	✓
Jill reports to Bill	
James reports to Jill	
Nicky reports to Bill	
Nicky reports to Jill	
Bill reports to James	
Emily reports to Jill	

When there are conflicts in the workplace you could try to resolve some issues yourself but others will have to be referred to your line manager.

(c) **Which of the following issues would you try to resolve yourself and which would you refer to your line manager?**

Issue	Resolve myself ✓	Refer to line manager ✓
Your line manager has asked you to complete a calculation of wage deductions. However, having started to look at the calculation, it is more complex than you thought and you do not feel you have had enough training to be able to perform it.		
You suspect a colleague has been setting up fictitious employees on the payroll in order to commit fraud.		
Your colleague has asked you to swap your work for the afternoon with her work, as yours looks more 'exciting'. However, you do not know how to carry out her tasks.		
You feel you are being bullied by a colleague.		

Task 11

Which of the following information provided by the accounting function can help the organisation maintain its solvency?

	✓
Produce a cash budget	
Produce a profit statement	
Ensure tax bills are paid on time	
Ensure inventory is kept at maximum levels	
Ensure receivables pay on time	
Monitor the cash budget	

Task 12

An accounts assistant works 9:00am to 5:00pm with an hour for lunch at 1:00pm. He has the following routine duties (duration of tasks are in brackets):

- Open the morning post (30 minutes)

- Pass any cheques received to the cashier (30 minutes)

- Enter sales invoices/credit notes daily in batches into computer system by midday (2 hours)

- Match and check purchase invoices to goods received notes daily and pass them all to the accountant for authorisation (6 minutes per invoice) (see related information that follows on the deadline for this)

- File sales invoices/credit notes (between 1 and 2 hours of filing)

Today is Friday 27 September and, having already opened the post and passed the cheques to the cashier, you get a telephone call from the accountant to say that one of your colleagues is not coming in today due to sickness. You now also need to enter the weekly purchase invoices into the computer today (which should only take an hour). Another colleague, who is back in the office this afternoon (2:00pm), needs to review a list of these invoices before the end of the day for forecasting purposes. The list is generated from the computer system you are entering the invoices into.

You have 20 purchase invoices that need to be matched to (and checked against) GRNs before the end of the day ready for authorisation first thing on Monday.

Decide on the order you would carry out the tasks included in the picklist.

Order	Task	
1st task		▼
2nd task		▼
3rd task		▼
4th task		▼

Picklist:

Enter sales invoices/credit notes into computer system

Enter weekly purchase invoices into the computer

Filing

Match purchase invoices to goods received notes and pass to the accountant for authorisation

Task 13

Your name is Justine Spring and you have recently been employed as an accounts assistant by Reeves Ltd, a company which produces and sells a variety of educational children's toys.

The job description below was given to you when you joined the company and was discussed with the HR Manager.

JOB DESCRIPTION	
Job title:	Accounts Assistant
Summary:	General financial and management accounting duties
Job content:	Enter daily sales invoices into computer
	Enter daily cash/cheque receipts into computer
	Enter daily cash/cheque payments into computer
	Prepare monthly bank reconciliation
	Deal with daily petty cash claims
	Enter petty cash details in computer weekly
	Assist in preparation of weekly payroll
	Other ad hoc financial/management accounting tasks
Reports to:	Accountant – Patrick Fellows
Hours:	9:00am to 5:30pm Monday to Friday
	1 hour for lunch
Training:	Necessary training to be provided
Prepared by:	HR Manager

Drag and drop choice

Enter your daily, weekly and monthly routine tasks using the table.

Daily tasks	
Weekly tasks	
Monthly tasks	

The drag and drop choices are:

Assist in preparation of payroll
Deal with petty cash claims
Enter cash/cheque receipts into the computer
Enter sales invoices into the computer
Prepare bank reconciliation
Enter petty cash details into the computer
Enter cash/cheque payments into computer
Other ad hoc accounting tasks

Task 14

(a) [_____ ▼] is **NOT** an advantage of working in a team **rather than as an individual.**

Picklist:

Additional resources
Communication
Independence
Inspiration
Motivation

(b) **If you disagree with a decision being made, and wish to influence the decision maker, what style of communication should you use to communicate with him or her?**

	✓
Aggressive	
Passive	
Argumentative	
Assertive	

···

Task 15

In the context of setting personal development objectives and using the picklist that follows the table below, determine which element of the SMART framework is being described.

Description	Element of SMART
Objectives must be achievable using available time and other resources	▼
Objectives must be formulated such that the achievement of them can be evaluated	▼
Objectives must be set within a specific timescale	▼
Development objectives must not be general	▼
Must be approved by the appropriate manager	▼

Picklist:

Agreed
Measurable
Realistic
Specific
Time-bounded

···

Task 16

Match the following learning needs (on the left) with an appropriate approach (on the right).

Need	Approach

Need	Approach
An employee wants to ensure that she is aware of the latest rules under the Data Protection Act	Training course
An accounts clerk wishes to improve in the use of double-entry bookkeeping and computer spreadsheets	Internet research
An accounts clerk wishes to improve his participation in team meetings	Experiential learning

Task 17

Which of these might (or might be thought to) affect the objectivity of providers of professional accounting services?

	✓
Failure to keep up to date on CPD	
A personal financial interest in the client's affairs	
Being negligent or reckless with the accuracy of the information provided to the client	

Task 18

Put the four steps of the problem-solving methodology or 'conceptual framework' for ethical conduct into the correct order:

Apply safeguards to eliminate or reduce the threat to an acceptable level	▼
Evaluate the seriousness of the threat	▼
Discontinue the action or relationship giving rise to the threat	▼
Identify a potential threat to a fundamental ethical principle	▼

Picklist:

1, 2, 3, 4

Assessment objective 2 – Bookkeeping Transactions

Task 19

There are three payments to be entered in the credit side of Gold's cash book during one week.

Cash purchases listing

Suppliers paid in cash	Net £	VAT £	Gross £
Mendip plc	315	63	378

Trade payables listing

Credit suppliers paid by cheque	Amount paid £
Landa Ltd	1,950
Bebe and Co	726

(a) **Enter the details from the cash purchases listing and the trade payables listing into the credit side of the cash book shown below and total each column.**

Cash book – credit side

Details	Cash £	Bank £	VAT £	Trade payables £	Cash purchases £
Balance b/f		2,312			
▼					
▼					
▼					
Total					

Picklist:

Bank
Bebe and Co
Cash
Cash purchases
Landa Ltd
Mendip plc
Trade payables
VAT

The debit side of the cash book shows the cash balance brought forward at the beginning of the week was £200 and a further £319 has been received during the week.

(b) Using your answer to (a) above, calculate the cash balance.

£ _____

The debit side of the cash book shows the total amount of money banked during the week was £1,964.

(c) Using your answer to (a) above, calculate the bank balance. If your calculations show that the bank account is overdrawn, your answer should start with a minus sign, for example –123.

£ _____

Task 20

Gold's cash book is both a book of prime entry and part of the double entry bookkeeping system. These are the totals of the columns in the credit site of the cash book at the end of a month.

Cash-book – credit side

Details	Cash £	Bank £	VAT £	Trade payables £	Cash purchases £	Bank charges £
Totals	1,590	10,948	265	10,900	1,325	48

(a) What will be the FOUR entries in the general ledger?

General ledger

Account name	Amount £	Debit	Credit
▼			
▼			
▼			
▼			

Picklist:

Bank
Bank charges
Cash
Cash purchases
Cash sales
Details
Purchases ledger control
Sales ledger control
Totals
Trade payables
VAT

One of the bank payments to trade payables was to D B Franks for £264.

(b)   What will be the entry in the purchases ledger?

Purchases ledger

Account name	Amount £	Debit	Credit
▼			

Picklist:

Bank
D B Franks
Gold
Purchases
Purchases ledger
Purchases ledger control
Sales
Sales ledger
Sales ledger control
Trade payables

Task 21

Below is the list of balances to be transferred to the trial balance.

Place the figures in the debit or credit column, as appropriate, and total each column. Do not enter figures with decimal places in this task and do not enter a zero in the empty column.

Trial balance as at 30 June

Account name	Amount £	Debit £	Credit £
Miscellaneous expenses	2,116		
Bank interest received	199		
Bank interest paid	342		
Petty cash control	175		
Office expenses	3,793		
Motor expenses	1,118		
Loan from bank	15,000		
Rent and rates	3,000		
Motor vehicles	37,650		
Sales	198,575		
Purchases returns	875		
Sales ledger control	128,331		
Bank (overdraft)	2,246		
Purchases ledger control	55,231		
VAT (owing to HM Revenue & Customs)	4,289		
Wages	37,466		
Purchases	88,172		
Capital	25,748		
Totals			

Task 22

The following account is in the sales ledger at the close of day on 30 June.

(a) Insert the balance carried down together with date and details.

(b) Insert the totals.

(c) Insert the balance brought down together with date and details.

J B Mills

Date 20XX	Details	Amount £	Date 20XX	Details	Amount £
1 Jun	Balance b/f	1,585	22 Jun	Bank	678
11 Jun	Invoice 1269	1,804	29 Jun	Credit note 049	607
▼	▼		▼	▼	
	Total			Total	
▼	▼		▼	▼	

Picklist:

30 Jun
1 July
Balance b/d
Balance c/d
Gold
J B Mills

Task 23

Gold started a new business, J Gems, on 1 July with the following assets and liabilities.

Assets and liabilities	£
Motor vehicle	22,615
Loan from bank	10,000
Inventories	9,881
Cash at bank	3,224

(a) **Show the accounting equation on 1 July by inserting the appropriate figures.**

Assets £	Liabilities £	Capital £

On 8 July the new business had the following assets and liabilities.

Assets and liabilities	£
Motor vehicle	22,615
Loan from bank	10,000
Inventories	8,326
Cash at bank	4,922
Trade receivables	7,600
Trade payables	1,270

(b) **Show the accounting equation on 8 July by inserting the appropriate figures.**

Assets £	Liabilities £	Capital £

(c) **Show whether the transactions of J Gems are classified as capital income, revenue income, capital expenditure or revenue expenditure by linking the transactions on the left hand side to the appropriate right hand box.**

Transactions	Income/Expenditure
Received cash for goods sold	
Purchased a motor vehicle for cash	Capital income
Purchased goods for resale for cash	Revenue income
Received a cheque from a trade receivable	Capital expenditure
Purchased goods for resale on credit	Revenue expenditure
Received cash from owner	

The goods that J Gems have bought on credit have been entered in the purchases day book.

(d) Is the purchases day book part of the double entry bookkeeping system?

	✓
Yes	
No	

All of J Gems' customers have a customer account code. The codes are made up of the first three letters of the customer's name, followed by the number of the ledger page allocated to each customer in that alphabetical group.

J Gems now has two new customers, MBJ Ltd and Portman and Co.

(e) Insert the relevant account code in the coding list below for each of the two new customers.

Customer name	Customer account code
Avion Ltd	AVI01
Blakely plc	BLA01
Brandon and Co	BRA02
Fellows Designs	FEL01
Nailer and Co	NAI01
MBJ Ltd	
Patel Products	PAT01
Pound plc	POU02
Pickford Ltd	PIC03
Portman and Co	
TJK Ltd	TJK01

Task 24

For each of the following transactions state whether they are cash or credit transactions.

	Cash transaction ✓	Credit transaction ✓
Purchase of goods for £500 payable by cheque in one week's time		
Arranging a banker's draft for the purchase of a new computer		
Sale of goods to a customer on account		
Sale of goods to a customer who paid by credit card at the time of the transaction		
Purchase of goods where payment is due in three weeks' time		

Task 25

On your desk is a pile of sales invoices that have already had the price of the goods entered onto them and been totalled.

You now have to calculate and deduct the 15% trade discount that is allowed on each of these invoices.

Goods total £	Trade discount £	Net total £
542.60		
107.50		
98.40		
257.10		
375.00		

Task 26

There is a further pile of invoices which have the net total entered for which you are required to calculate the VAT charge at 20% and the invoice total.

Net total £	VAT £	Gross total £
236.40		
372.10		
85.60		
159.40		
465.30		

Task 27

The following purchases have been made for cash inclusive of VAT at 20%.

Calculate the amount of VAT on each purchase and the net amount of the purchase:

Gross total £	VAT £	Net total £
277.24		
163.42		
49.74		
108.28		
69.42		
831.20		

Task 28

Sugar Solutions is a small business that manufactures a variety of confectionery which it sells directly to shops. During January 20XX the following credit sales to customers took place:

Invoice No. 7541 to Watsons Ltd £547 plus VAT
Invoice No. 7542 to Harrison £660 plus VAT
Invoice No. 7543 to Valu Shopping £346 plus VAT
Invoice No. 7544 to Fishers £328 plus VAT
Invoice No. 7545 to Harrison £548 plus VAT
Invoice No. 7546 to Villa Discount £141 plus VAT
Invoice No. 7547 to Valu Shopping £416 plus VAT
Invoice No. 7548 to Watsons Ltd £238 plus VAT
Invoice No. 7549 to Fishers £305 plus VAT

You are required to:

(a)   Enter these transactions into the sales day book given below.

(b)   Cast the columns of the sales day book and check that they cross cast.

Sales day book

Customer		Invoice number	Total £	VAT £	Net £
	▼				
	▼				
	▼				
	▼				
	▼				
	▼				
	▼				
	▼				
	▼				
	▼				

Picklist:

Fishers
Harrison
Valu Shopping
Villa Discount
Watsons

Cross-cast check:

	£
Net	
VAT	
Total	

Task 29

You have been given an extract from your organisation's purchases day book in respect of credit transactions taking place in June. No entries have yet been made in the ledgers.

Both suppliers charge VAT on sales.

You are required to complete the purchases day book and state what the entries will be in the purchases ledger.

Purchases day book

Date 20XX	Details	Invoice number	Total £	VAT £	Net £
30 June	Bramley Ltd	7623			2,571.00
30 June	Russett & Co	0517	2,400.00		
	Totals				

Purchases ledger

Account name	Amount £	Debit ✓	Credit ✓
▼			
▼			

Picklist:

Bramley Ltd
Russett & Co
Net
Purchases
Purchases ledger control
Purchases returns
Sales
Sales ledger control
Sales returns
Total
VAT

Task 30

Your organisation has received a statement from a supplier which shows that, as at the end of June 20XX, you owed the supplier £2,876. The purchases ledger account for this supplier shows that at that date you only owed £1,290.

Which of the following items would explain the difference?

	✓
You have requested a credit note from the supplier for £1,586 which you have not yet received.	
You sent a cheque for £1,586 to the supplier on 30 June 20XX.	
You ordered some items from the supplier on 30 June for £1,586 but the goods have not yet been delivered and an invoice has not yet been raised.	

Task 31

Matilda sells machine tools. The following is a summary of her transactions with Frampton Ltd, a new credit customer.

£656 re invoice 1540 of 15 September
£742 re invoice 1560 of 29 September
£43 re credit note 89 of 3 October
£1,235 re invoice 1580 of 10 October
Cheque for £682 received 15 October

Complete the statement of account below. Enter all amounts as a positive value.

		Matilda's Machinery 1 North Street Westbury, WE11 9SD	
To: Frampton Ltd			Date: 31 October 20XX

Date 20XX	Details	Transaction amount £	Outstanding amount £
	▼		
	▼		
	▼		
	▼		
	▼		

Picklist:

Cheque
Credit note 89
Invoice 1540
Invoice 1560
Invoice 1580

Task 32

On the first day of every month cash is drawn from the bank to restore the petty cash imprest level to £75.

A summary of petty cash transactions during November is shown below:

Opening balance on 1 November	£27
Cash from bank on 1 November	£48
Expenditure during month	£21

(a) What will be the amount required to restore the imprest level on 1 December?

£

(b) Will the receipt from the bank on 1 December be a debit or credit entry in the petty cash book?

	✓
Debit	
Credit	

Assessment objective 3 – Bookkeeping Controls/Elements of Costing

Task 33

Gold has started a new business, Dee Designs, and a new set of accounts is to be opened. A partially completed journal to record the opening entries is shown below.

Complete the journal by showing whether each amount will be a debit or a credit entry.

The Journal

Account name	Amount £	Debit ✓	Credit ✓
Capital	4,780		
Office expenses	1,927		
Sales	8,925		
Purchases	4,212		
Commission received	75		
Discounts received	54		
Cash at bank	1,814		
Petty cash	180		
Loan from bank	5,000		
Motor expenses	372		
Motor vehicles	9,443		
Other expenses	886		

Journal to record opening entries of new business.

Task 34

A payment through the bank of £12,265 for new computer equipment has been entered in the accounting records as £12,565. (Ignore VAT.)

(a) **Record the journal entries needed in the general ledger to remove the incorrect entry.**

Account name		Amount £	Debit ✓	Credit ✓
	▼			
	▼			

Picklist:

Bank
Cash
Computer equipment
Purchases
Suspense

(b) **Record the journal entries needed in the general ledger to record the correct entry.**

Account name		Amount £	Debit ✓	Credit ✓
	▼			
	▼			

Picklist:

Bank
Cash
Computer equipment
Purchases
Suspense

Task 35

Gold's trial balance included a suspense account. All of the bookkeeping errors have now been traced and the journal entries shown below have been recorded.

Journal entries

Account name	Debit £	Credit £
Commission received	545	
Rent received		545
Suspense	985	
Legal fees		985
General repairs	3,667	
Suspense		3,667

Post the journal entries to the general ledger accounts below by writing the details and amounts in the relevant accounts.

Commission received

Details	Amount £	Details	Amount £

Rent received

Details	Amount £	Details	Amount £

Suspense

Details	Amount £	Details	Amount £
Balance b/f	2,682		

Legal fees

Details	Amount £	Details	Amount £

General repairs

Details	Amount £	Details	Amount £

Details and amounts:

| Commission received |

| General repairs |

| Legal fees |

| Rent received |

| Suspense |

| Suspense |

| 545 | 545 |

| 985 | 985 |

| 3,667 | 3,667 |

Task 36

On 30 June Gold extracted an initial trial balance which did not balance, and a suspense account was opened with a £962 debit balance. On 1 July journal entries were prepared to correct the errors that had been found, and clear the suspense account. The journal entries to correct the errors, and the list of balances in the initial trial balance, are shown below.

Re-draft the trial balance by placing the figures in the debit or credit column. You should take into account the journal entries which will clear the suspense account. Do not enter your figures with decimal places in this task and do not enter a zero in the empty column.

Journal entries

Account name	Debit £	Credit £
Cash	812	
Suspense		812
Bank	812	
Suspense		812

Account name	Debit £	Credit £
Suspense	331	
Sales		331
Purchases		331
Suspense	331	

Trial balance

Account names	Balances extracted on 30 June £	Debit balances at 1 July £	Credit balances at 1 July £
Capital	20,774		
Motor vehicles	47,115		
Cash at bank	11,923		
Cash	200		
Sales ledger control	120,542		
Purchases ledger control	60,224		
VAT (owing to HM Revenue and Customs)	7,916		
Office expenses	3,216		
Sales	207,426		
Purchases	99,250		
Motor expenses	4,310		
Other expenses	8,822		
Totals			

Task 37

The bank statement and cash book for September are shown below.

Bank statement

Date	Details	Paid out £	Paid in £	Balance £
20XX				
01 Sep	Balance b/f			4,104 D
01 Sep	BACS transfer – CDL Ltd		4,996	
01 Sep	Cheque 001499	1,015		123 D
04 Sep	Counter credit		2,240	2,117 C
12 Sep	Cheque 001500	486		1,631 C
22 Sep	CHAPS transfer – Conway Legal		37,400	
22 Sep	Cheque 001505	819		38,212 C
27 Sep	Cheque 001501	209		
27 Sep	Counter credit		1,081	
27 Sep	Cheque 001504	1,618		37,466 C
	D = Debit C = Credit			

Cash book

Date 20XX	Details	Bank £	Date 20XX	Cheque Number	Details	Bank £
01 Sep	CDL Ltd	4,996	01 Sep		Balance b/f	5,119
04 Sep	Gifford Ltd	2,240	02 Sep	001500	Babbing Ltd	486
22 Sep	Kington Ltd	3,970	08 Sep	001501	Vym plc	209
22 Sep	Conway Legal	37,400	12 Sep	001502	Newton West	195
27 Sep	Fairway Ltd	1,081	12 Sep	001503	Welland Ltd	234
			18 Sep	001504	Hawes Ltd	1,618
			18 Sep	001505	Halthorpe Ltd	819
			18 Sep	001506	Roman plc	316

Identify the FOUR transactions that are included in the cash book but missing from the bank statement and complete the bank reconciliation statement below as at 30 September.

Bank reconciliation statement as at 30 September 20XX		£
Balance as per bank statement		
Add:		
	▼	
Total to add		
Less:		
	▼	
	▼	
	▼	
Total to subtract		
Balance as per cash book		

Picklist:

Babbing Ltd
Balance b/f
Balance c/d
CDL Ltd
Cheque 001499
Conway Legal
Fairway Ltd
Gifford Ltd
Halthorpe Ltd
Hawes Ltd
Kington Ltd
Newton West
Roman plc
Vym plc
Welland Ltd

Task 38

The following is a summary of transactions with credit customers during the month of July.

(a) **Show whether each entry will be a debit or credit in the sales ledger control account in the general ledger.**

Sales ledger control account

Details	Amount £	Debit ✓	Credit ✓
Balance owing from credit customers at 1 July	101,912		
Money received from credit customers	80,435		
Irrecoverable debts	228		
Goods sold to credit customers	70,419		
Goods returned by credit customers	2,237		

The following is a summary of transactions with credit suppliers during the month of July.

(b) **Show whether each entry will be a debit or credit in the purchases ledger control account in the general ledger.**

Purchases ledger control account

Details	Amount £	Debit ✓	Credit ✓
Balance owing to credit suppliers at 1 July	61,926		
Journal debit to correct an error	550		
Goods returned to credit suppliers	1,128		
Purchases from credit suppliers	40,525		
Payments made to credit suppliers	45,763		

At the beginning of September the following balances were in the sales ledger.

Credit customers	Balances	
	Amount £	Debit/Credit
CTC Ltd	11,122	Debit
J B Estates	8,445	Debit
Koo Designs	23,119	Debit
PJB Ltd	1,225	Credit
Probyn pic	19,287	Debit
Yen Products	4,302	Debit

(c) **What should be the balance of the sales ledger control account in order for it to reconcile with the total of the balances in the sales ledger?**

Balance	✓
Credit balance b/d on 1 September of £65,050	
Debit balance b/d on 1 September of £65,050	
Credit balance b/d on 1 September of £67,500	
Debit balance b/d on 1 September of £67,500	

(d) **Show whether each of the following statements is true or false.**

Statements	True ✓	False ✓
The purchases ledger control account enables a business to identify how much is owing to credit suppliers in total.		
The total of the balances in the purchases ledger should reconcile with the balance of the sales ledger control account.		

Task 39

Below is a summary of transactions to be recorded in the VAT control account.

Transactions	Amount £
VAT owing from HM Revenue and Customs at 1 June	13,146
VAT total in the purchases day-book	19,220
VAT total in the sales day-book	31,197
VAT total in the purchases returns day-book	2,465
VAT total in the sales returns day-book	1,779
VAT on cash sales	1,910
VAT on petty cash payments	98
VAT refund received from HM Revenue and Customs	7,131
VAT on irrecoverable debts written off	950
VAT on the sale of office equipment	200

(a) **Show how each of the transactions will be recorded in the VAT control account in the general ledger by inputting each transaction below to the appropriate side of the VAT control account.**

VAT control

Details	Amount £	Details	Amount £

Transactions:

Balance b/f – owing from HMRC	13,146
Purchases	19,220
Sales	31,197
Purchases returns	2,465
Sales returns	1,779
Cash sales	1,910
Petty cash	98
VAT refund	7,131
Irrecoverable debts	950
Office equipment sold	200

The VAT return shows there is an amount owing from HM Revenue and Customs of £7,710.

(b) Does the balance on the VAT control account in part (a) also show that £7,710 is owing from HM Revenue and Customs?

	✓
Yes	
No	

(c) Identify which ONE of the following sentences is true.

	✓
The VAT control account is used to record the VAT amount of transactions and to help prepare the VAT return.	
The VAT control account is used to record the VAT amount of transactions but has no connection with the VAT return.	

Task 40

Gold uses different forms of payment.

(a) **Show the most appropriate form of payment for each transaction below by linking each transaction on the left hand side with the appropriate right hand box.**

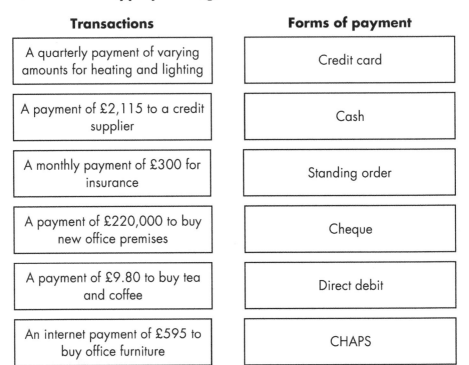

Transactions	Forms of payment
A quarterly payment of varying amounts for heating and lighting	Credit card
A payment of £2,115 to a credit supplier	Cash
A monthly payment of £300 for insurance	Standing order
A payment of £220,000 to buy new office premises	Cheque
A payment of £9.80 to buy tea and coffee	Direct debit
An internet payment of £595 to buy office furniture	CHAPS

(b) **Show whether the following statements are true or false.**

Statements	True ✓	False ✓
Purchases made using a debit card will result in funds being immediately transferred from Gold's bank account.		
Before accepting a payment by cheque from a new customer, Gold should ask the bank if there are sufficient funds in the customer's bank account.		

Task 41

Would each of the following transactions appear as a payment in or a payment out on a business's bank statement?

Transaction	Payment out ✓	Payment in ✓
£725 paid into the bank		
Direct debit for £47		
Cheque payment of £124.60		
Interest charged on the overdraft		
BACS payment for wages		

Task 42

The bank statement and cash book for November are shown below.

(a) **Check the bank statement against the cash book and enter:**

- **Any transactions into the cash book as needed**
- **The cash book balance carried down at 30 November and brought down at 1 December**

Bank statement

Date	Details	Paid out £	Paid in £	Balance £
03 Nov	Balance b/f			9,136 C
07 Nov	Cheque 110870	5,175		3,961 C
17 Nov	Cheque 110872	2,250		1,711 C
21 Nov	Cheque 110865	2,361		650 D
	Direct Debit – Insurance	500		1,150 D
21 Nov	Counter Credit – BBT Ltd		8,000	6,850 C
24 Nov	Counter Credit – Welders Ltd		2,555	9,405 C
	Direct Debit – Chainsaw Ltd	88		9,317 C
25 Nov	Cheque 110871	1,234		8,083 C

D = Debit   C = Credit

Cash book

Date	Details	Bank £	Date	Cheque number/ Direct debit	Details	Bank £
01 Nov	Balance b/f	6,775	03 Nov	110870	Robots & Co	5,175
24 Nov	Bishops Ltd	1,822	03 Nov	110871	W Bevan	1,234
24 Nov	Griplock Ltd	7,998	06 Nov	110872	Fishhooks Ltd	2,250
	▼		10 Nov	110873	Sanding Supplies	275
	▼		17 Nov	110874	Waders & Co	76
	▼			▼	▼	
	▼			▼	▼	
	▼			▼	▼	
	▼			▼	▼	
	▼			▼	▼	

Picklist:

Balance b/d
Balance c/d
Bishops Ltd
BBT Ltd
Chainsaw ltd
Counter credit
Direct debit
Fishhooks Ltd
Griplock Ltd
Insurance
Robots & Co
Sanding Supplies
W Bevan
Waders & Co
Welders Ltd

(b) **Using the information from the cash book and bank statement, prepare a bank reconciliation statement as at 30 November.**

Bank reconciliation statement as at 30 November	£	£
Balance per bank statement		
Add:		
▼		
▼		
Total to add		
Less:		
▼		
▼		
Total to subtract		
Balance as per cash book		

Picklist:

Bishops Ltd
Cheque 110865
Counter credit
Direct debit
Fishhooks Ltd
Griplock Ltd
Robots & Co
Sanding Supplies
W Bevan
Waders & Co

Task 43

Your organisation is not registered for VAT. This is a summary of transactions with credit customers during April.

	£
Balance owing at 1 April	27,321
Goods sold	11,267
Goods returned	1,934
Payments received by cheque	10,006
Irrecoverable debts	742

Record these transactions in the sales ledger control account and show the balance carried down.

Sales ledger control

Details	£	Details	£
▼		▼	
▼		▼	
▼		▼	
▼		▼	
▼		▼	

Picklist:

Balance b/f
Balance c/d
Bank
Irrecoverable debts
Discounts received
Purchases
Purchases returns
Sales
Sales returns

Task 44

Your organisation is not registered for VAT. This is a summary of transactions with credit suppliers for the month of April.

	£
Balance owing at 1 April	6,547
Goods purchased	9,317
Goods returned	751
Payments made by cheque	8,653
Discounts received	481

Record these transactions in the purchases ledger control account and show the balance carried down.

Purchases ledger control

Details		£	Details		£
▼			▼		
▼			▼		
▼			▼		
▼			▼		
▼			▼		

Picklist:

Balance b/f
Balance c/d
Bank
Discounts received
Purchases
Purchases returns
Sales
Sales returns

Task 45

When reconciling sales ledger and purchases ledger control accounts to the list of balances from the subsidiary ledgers, would the following errors affect the relevant control account, the list of balances or both?

	Control account ✓	List of balances ✓	Both ✓
Invoice entered into the sales day book as £540 instead of £450			
Purchases day book overcast by £1,100			
An invoice taken as £430 instead of £330 when being posted to the customer's account			
Incorrect balancing of a subsidiary ledger account			
A purchases return not entered into the purchases returns day book			

Task 46

The balance on a business's sales ledger control account at 31 December was £12,467. However the list of balances in the sales ledger totalled £11,858. The difference was investigated and the following errors were discovered:

(i)   The sales returns day book was undercast by £100.

(ii) A payment from one customer had been correctly entered into the cash book as £340 but had been entered into the sales ledger as £430.

(iii) An irrecoverable debt of £250 had been written off in the sales ledger but had not been entered into the general ledger accounts.

(iv) A balance of £169 due from one customer had been omitted from the list of sales ledger balances.

You are required to write up the corrected sales ledger control account and to reconcile this to the corrected list of sales ledger balances.

Sales ledger control

Details	£	Details	£
▼		▼	
▼		▼	
▼		▼	
▼		▼	
▼		▼	

Picklist:

Balance b/f
Balance c/d
Bank
Discounts received
Irrecoverable debts
Purchases
Purchases returns
Sales
Sales returns

	£
Sales ledger list of balances	
Error	
Error	
Amended list of balances	
Amended control account balance	

Task 47

An organisation has started a new business and a new set of accounts is to be opened. A partially completed journal to record the opening entries is shown below.

Complete the journal by showing whether each amount will be a debit or a credit entry.

Journal

Account name	Amount £	Debit ✓	Credit ✓
Capital	20,000		
Furniture and fittings	5,315		
Sales	107,318		
Motor vehicles	10,109		
Cash at bank	15,000		
Purchases	96,120		
Sales returns	750		
Purchases ledger control	27,238		
Sales ledger control	51,759		
Loan from bank	17,000		
Motor expenses	1,213		
VAT (owed to HM Revenue and Customs)	8,710		

Task 48

Nordeste Ltd is in business as a manufacturer of stationery.

(a) **Classify the following costs it incurred by element (material, labour or overhead) by putting a tick in the relevant column of the table below.**

Cost	Material ✓	Labour ✓	Overhead ✓
Insurance of office computers			
Ink cartridges used in the production of pens			
Wages of employees in the production department			
Card used to produce binders for notebooks			

(b) **Classify the following costs incurred by nature (direct or indirect) by putting a tick in the relevant column of the table below.**

Cost	Direct ✓	Indirect ✓
Insurance of factory		
Paper used in the manufacture of envelopes		
Salary of production manager		
Plastic used in the production of pens		

Task 49

Squench Ltd produces fruit drinks.

(a) **Classify the following costs incurred by function (production, administration, selling and distribution or finance) by putting a tick in the relevant column of the table below.**

Cost	Production ✓	Administration ✓	Selling and distribution ✓	Finance ✓
Fruit purchased for use in drinks				
Stationery provided to all departments				
Interest charged on bank loan				
Sales campaign				

(b) **Classify the following costs by their behaviour (fixed, variable or semi-variable) by putting a tick in the relevant column of the table below.**

Cost	Fixed ✓	Variable ✓	Semi-variable ✓
Employees in the bottling department paid on a piecework basis			
Annual consultancy charge for updating the website			
Sugar used in drinks			
Machinery hire consisting of a fixed rental charge and a usage charge			

Task 50

Workout Ltd produces and sells sports and leisurewear. It uses a numerical coding structure based on one profit centre and three cost centres as outlined in the first four columns of the table below. Each code has a sub-code so each transaction will be coded as ***/***.

You are required to classify the revenue and expense transactions shown in the transaction column of the table below using the code column for your answer.

Profit/Cost centre	Cost code	Sub-classification	Sub-code	Transaction	Code
Sales	120	Sportswear	075		
		Leisurewear	085		
Production	230	Direct cost	160	Sales of football shirts	
		Indirect cost	170	Cotton used in leisure shirts	
Administration	340	Direct cost	255	Cleaning materials used in factory	
		Indirect cost	265	Sales of casual shorts	
Selling and Distribution	450	Direct cost	340	Heating of administration offices	
		Indirect cost	350	Cost of advertising campaign	

Task 51

Firstglow Ltd has set up an investment centre for a project it is undertaking over a period of years. It uses an alpha coding system for its investments, revenues and costs and then further classifies numerically as outlined in the first four columns of the table below.

You are required to code the transactions listed in the transaction column of the table below using the code column for your answers. Each transaction should have a five character code.

Activity	Code	Nature of cost	Sub-code	Transaction	Code
Investments	IN	External	210	External funds used to set up investment	
		Internal	240	External contractor charge	
Revenues	RE	UK	320	Material used on project	
		Overseas	350	Salaries paid to employees	
Costs	CO	Material	420	Project revenue arising in the UK	
		Labour	530	Firstglow Ltd company funds invested in project	
		Overheads	640		

Task 52

The table below lists a number of costs.

(a) **Indicate whether the following costs are an overhead or not by putting a tick in the relevant column of the table below.**

Cost	Yes ✓	No ✓
Fee paid to an external accountant		
Salary of chief executive		
Wages of production workers making the product		

Havenport Ltd makes a single product. A production level of 75,000 units has the following costs:

Materials   50,000 kilos at £33 per kilo
Labour   40,000 hours at £22.50 per hour
Overheads £1,950,000

(b) **Complete the table below to show the unit product cost at the production level of 75,000 units.**

Element	Unit product cost £
Materials	
Labour	
Direct Cost	
Overheads	
Total	

Task 53

(a) Re-order the following costs into a manufacturing account format for the year ended 31 December. You should write out each item in the correct position on the list on the right side below. Note that where costs are not given you will need to determine these in part (b).

	£	Manufacturing account	£
Manufacturing cost			
Direct labour	144,000		
Cost of goods sold			
Cost of goods manufactured			
Closing inventory of finished goods	101,200		
Direct cost			
Opening inventory of raw materials	52,700		
Closing inventory of raw materials	48,100		
Closing inventory of work in progress	74,200		
Manufacturing overheads	237,400		
Direct materials used			
Opening inventory of finished goods	107,600		
Opening inventory of work in progress	72,400		
Purchase of raw materials	221,100		

(b) **Determine and enter the cost totals below, using your answer to part (a) to help you.**

Manufacturing account	£
Direct materials used	
Direct cost	
Manufacturing cost	
Cost of goods manufactured	
Cost of goods sold	

Task 54

You are told the opening inventory of a single raw material in the stores is 1,200 units at £6.00 per unit. During the month 1,800 units at £8.00 per unit are received and the following week 2,400 units are issued.

(a) **Identify the valuation method described in the statements below.**

Statement	FIFO ✓	LIFO ✓	AVCO ✓
The closing inventory is valued at £4,800			
The issue of 2,400 units is costed at £17,280			
The issue of 2,400 units is costed at £18,000			

You are told the opening inventory of a single raw material in the stores is 1,200 units at £6.00 per unit. During the month 1,800 units at £8.00 per unit are received and the following week 2,400 units are issued.

(b) **Identify whether the statements in the table below are true or false by putting a tick in the relevant column.**

Statement	True ✓	False ✓
AVCO values the closing inventory at £4,320		
FIFO costs the issue of 2,400 units at £16,900		
LIFO values the closing inventory at £3,600		

Task 55

A business has the following movements in a certain type of inventory into and out of its stores for the month of February.

Date	Receipts		Issues	
	Units	Cost	Units	Cost
4 Feb	1,000	£4,000		
7 Feb	500	£2,500		
11 Feb	2,000	£11,000		
19 Feb			2,100	
24 Feb	1,800	£11,700		

Complete the table below by entering the cost of issue and closing inventory values.

Method	Cost of issue on 19 February £	Closing inventory at 28 February £
FIFO		
LIFO		
AVCO		

Task 56

An employee is paid £8.00 an hour and is expected to make 25 units an hour.

Any excess production will be paid a bonus of 20p per unit.

(a) **Identify the following statements as being true or false by putting a tick in the relevant column of the table below.**

Statements	True ✓	False ✓
During a 36 hour week an employee produces 910 units and does not receive a bonus		
During a 40 hour week an employee produces 1,180 units and receives a bonus of £36		
During a 37 hour week an employee produces 980 units and receives total pay of £307		

Northcake Ltd pays a time-rate of £12.50 per hour for a 36-hour week.

Any employee working in excess of 36 hours per week is paid an overtime rate of £15.00 per hour.

(b) **Calculate the basic wage, overtime and gross wage for the week for the two employees in the table below. Note. If no overtime is paid you should enter 0 as the overtime for that employee.**

Employee	Hours worked	Basic wage £	Overtime £	Gross wage £
V. Chopra	40			
R. Silvai	43			

Task 57

Piecework is a method of paying labour.

Identify the following statements about the piecework method as either true or false by putting a tick in the relevant column of the table below.

Statement	True ✓	False ✓
Employees' pay will increase if more units are produced		
An employee is paid 45p per unit and earns £288 for a production of 640 units		
An employee who is paid £350 for a production of 875 units is paid 40p per unit		
Employees paid on a piecework basis will always earn an agreed total amount of pay		

Task 58

Fanfest Ltd uses a time-rate method with bonus to pay the employees in its factory. The time-rate used is £11.00 per hour and an employee is expected to produce 12 units per hour; anything over this and the employee is paid a bonus of 25p per unit.

Calculate the basic wage, bonus and gross wage for the week for the three employees in the table below. Note. If no bonus is paid you should enter 0 as the bonus for that employee in the table.

Employee	Hours worked	Units produced	Basic wage £	Bonus £	Gross wage £
L. Singh	42	500			
M. Barton	39	540			
S. Valencia	41	508			

Task 59

Johnson Ltd has the following actual results for the month of April which are to be compared to the budget:

Income   £40,000

Expenditure:

Materials   £15,000
Labour   £8,000
Overheads   £7,500

Enter the above data into the table below, calculate the variance for each item of income and expenditure, and determine whether it is adverse or favourable (enter A or F).

Income/Expenditure	Budget £	Actual £	Variance £	Adverse or Favourable (A or F)
Income	45,000			
Material	15,800			
Labour	9,000			
Overheads	8,800			

Assessment objective 4 – Work Effectively in Finance

Task 60

This is a draft of a letter to be addressed to Mrs Gray, a customer, to advise her of the results of your review of her account. The account information is as follows:

Account number	GR45276091
Credit limit	£5,000.00
Current balance	£4,752.50
Other information	Order placed yesterday, 25.08.XX, for £1,750 which cannot be sent due to the customer exceeding their credit limit.

Review the draft letter and identify EIGHT words or collections of letters or digits which are either spelt incorrectly or technically incorrect.

Acount GR45276091

Dear Mrs Gray,

Please find inclosed a current statement for your account. As you will see from the statement, the current account balance for your organisation is £4,725.50. I have been adviced that you have recently placed an order for goods to the value of £1,750. This order is currently on hold as the extra purchases will result in your credit limit of £5,000 being exceeded.

You are a highly valued customer and I notise that we have not reviewed your credit limit for a number of years. I would therefore suggest that we increase your credit limit to £7,000. If you consider this amount to be insufficient for your current needs please contact me and we can arrange a meeting to review your account.

I would appreciate it if you could make contact as soon as posible so that we can discuss the matter further. I shall be out of the office from next Thursday for a week so if you could contact me before then it would be helpful. I will arrange four the immediate delivery of your outstanding order as soon as I receive your agreement to the revised credit limit.

I look forward to hearing from you.

Yours faithfully

Task 61

(a) Last year the accounting function was restructured ahead of a wider organisational restructuring across all functions. To learn from the implementation of the changes, the Finance Director sent a questionnaire to all 30 staff within the finance function.

The Finance Director has asked you to review the responses to the five key statements and provide him with conclusions and recommendations which he can present to the other directors so that the rest of the organisation's restructuring goes as smoothly as possible.

Statement	Response		
	Number of staff who agreed	Number of staff who disagreed	Number of staff who did not answer
The company briefing explaining the process and timescales for the restructuring of the finance function helped reduce my concerns about the changes.	27	1	2
My manager kept staff fully informed of developments and changes during the restructuring.	4	24	2
My manager had the time to listen to staff concerns during the restructuring process.	6	16	8
The information provided prior to the restructuring in terms of job roles and responsibilities was helpful in identifying my own role and that of colleagues within the team.	20	7	3
The team building event which took place prior to the restructuring was helpful in getting to know other colleagues within the team.	25	2	3
The new team approach to working has resulted in more efficient working practices.	22	4	4

(i) **Identify from the statements below THREE conclusions and TWO recommendations that the Finance Director should present to the other directors so that staff stress during restructuring is kept to a minimum.**

	Conclusion ✓	Recommendation ✓
For most staff the company briefing explaining the process and timescales for the restructuring of the finance function helped reduce their concerns and the manager kept most staff fully informed of developments and changes during the restructuring.		
Most staff felt that their manager had the time to listen to their concerns during the restructuring process and most staff believe that the new team approach has resulted in increased efficiency of working practices.		
For the wider restructuring, managers need to be trained to ensure that they keep staff fully informed and up to date and that they have the time to listen to their staff's concerns.		
Information about job roles and responsibilities, provided to staff prior to the restructuring, was helpful to staff in positioning both their own and colleagues' roles within their team. However, the team building event prior to restructuring was not considered helpful in enabling staff to get to know colleagues within their team.		
Most staff felt that their manager did not keep them fully informed of developments and changes during the restructuring and most staff believe that the new team approach has resulted in increased efficiency of working practices.		

	Conclusion ✓	Recommendation ✓
The team building event held before the finance function restructuring should not be implemented across the organisation as finance staff did not consider it to be helpful in getting to know colleagues within their team.		
For most staff the company briefing explaining the process and timescales for the restructuring of the finance function helped reduce their concerns and the team building event prior to restructuring was considered helpful in enabling staff to get to know colleagues within their team.		
The company briefing explaining the process and timescales for the restructuring of the finance function and the team building event should be features of the wider organisational restructuring as most staff considered they were helpful.		
Information about job roles and responsibilities, provided to staff prior to the restructuring, was helpful to staff in identifying both their own and colleagues' roles within their team. However, most felt that their manager did not have the time to listen to their concerns during the restructuring process.		

(ii) **Select which of the following would be the most suitable title for this report.**

	✓
Results of the questionnaire	
A review of the communications strategy	
A review of the finance function	
A review of restructuring of the finance function	
A review of staff perceptions of their manager	

(b) **Identify which TWO of the following would occur before the introduction section of a business report:**

	✓
Appendices	
Recommendations	
Main body	
Conclusion	
Executive summary	
Title	

Task 62

The following is a report, file name 'PDBEOct.xls', that you have completed detailing expenses for the production department for the month of October.

Expenses	October Budget £	October Actual £
Wages – basic pay	18,000	16,500
Wages – overtime rate	0	3,000
Protective clothing	200	150
Machine oil	500	650
Cleaning materials	300	295
Sundries	1,000	1,050
Total expenses	20,000	21,645

Your manager has asked you to email the Production Manager, John Uwaifo (j.uwaifo@GCCS.com), to advise him of the differences between budget and actual spend on his expenses for the month of October. You must attach the file you have completed to the email.

(a) **Complete the email below by inserting the email address of the recipient and the file name of any attachments and selecting TWO correct paragraphs that should be inserted into the main body of the email.**

From:	AATstudent@GCCS.com
To:	
Subject:	Production expenses October actual compared to budget
Attached:	

Hello John

> **Paragraph 1**

> **Paragraph 2**

Regards

AAT student

	Paragraph 1 ✓	Paragraph 2 ✓
Whilst you spent more on wages at the basic rate of pay, you spent less than budget on wages at overtime rate. You spent more than budget on your protective clothing, machine oil and cleaning materials. You spent less than budget on sundry expenses. I hope you find this information useful, if you require any further analysis please do not hesitate to contact me.		
Following the production of the latest month-end report, see attached, I herewith provide you with an analysis of your expenses paid in the month of October. Overall you spent less than budget on your total expenses by £1,645 but this is made up of different expenses in some of which you exceeded budget and in some of which you spent less than budget.		

	Paragraph 1 ✓	Paragraph 2 ✓
Whilst you spent less on wages at the basic rate of pay you spent more than budget on wages at overtime rate. You spent less than budget on your protective clothing and cleaning materials. You spent more than budget on machine oil and sundry expenses. I hope you find this information useful, if you require any further analysis please do not hesitate to contact me.		
Following the production of the latest month-end report, see attached, I herewith provide you with an analysis of your expenses paid in the month of October. Overall you spent more than budget on your total expenses by £1,465 but this is made up of different expenses in some of which you exceeded budget and in some of which you spent less than budget.		
Whilst you spent less on wages at the basic rate of pay you spent less than budget on wages at overtime rate. You spent more than budget on your protective clothing, machine oil and cleaning materials. You spent less than budget on sundry expenses. I hope you find this information useful, if you require any further analysis please do not hesitate to contact me.		
Following the production of the latest month-end report, see attached, I herewith provide you with an analysis of your expenses paid in the month of October. Overall you spent more than budget on your total expenses by £1,645 but this is made up of different expenses in some of which you exceeded budget and in some of which you spent less than budget.		

(b)   Identify whether the following statements are true or false.

It is not necessary to proofread emails if they are sent to people within your organisation but external emails must always be proofread.

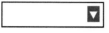

The main problem with sending information in an email is that irrespective of the file size only one file may be attached to an email.

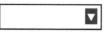

Picklist:

True
False

....

Task 63

The following is an income and expenditure statement for the Faculty of Business and Finance at a local college for the first half of the financial year. The Finance Director has asked you to analyse the results shown in the statement and provide him with conclusions and recommendations which he can present to the College Principal.

Income and expenditure statement	Actual £	Budget £	% Variance +/−	Comments
Income				
Full-time course fees	301,000	350,000	−14%	Lower numbers of students than expected registered for full-time courses.
Part-time course fees	58,125	46,500	+25%	The number of students registering for the new AAT part-time study programme exceeds budget.
One-day course fees	7,800	13,000	−40%	A reduction in marketing activity led to insufficient numbers of students to enable the planned practical bookkeeping course and revision courses to be run.
Total income	**366,835**	**409,350**		

Income and expenditure statement	Actual £	Budget £	% Variance +/−	Comments
Expenditure				
Basic salaries – Full-time staff	89,250	105,000	−15%	Saving is a result of covering one vacant full-time post with part-time hours for the whole period.
Basic salaries – Part-time staff	37,440	31,200	+20%	Overspend is a result of covering the full-time vacancy with additional part-time hours.
Student registration fees	22,500	25,000	−10%	Lower numbers of students for full-time and one-day courses.
Student exam fees	28,620	27,000	+6%	Lower numbers of full-time registrations compensated for by increases in part-time registrations.
Teaching materials	9,500	10,000	−5%	Lower numbers of full-time students.
Books	15,000	20,000	−25%	Obtained a bulk ordering discount on new accounting textbooks.
Total expenditure	**202,310**	**218,200**		

(a) (i) **Identify, from the statements below, THREE conclusions and TWO recommendations that the Finance Director should present to the College Principal.**

Statement	Conclusion ✓	Recommendation ✓
The reduction in actual full-time course fee income when compared to the budget is fully offset by the amount that the actual part-time course fee income exceeds budget.		

Statement	Conclusion ✓	Recommendation ✓
The new AAT study programme has been successful in increasing actual part-time course fee income and exceeding the budget, but the actual one-day course fee income is less than the budget.		
The faculty has been successful in reducing the actual cost of books by 25% when compared to the budget, but has overspent on the cost of teaching materials by 5% when compared to the budget.		
The reduction in actual full-time course fee income when compared to the budget is only partially offset by the amount that the actual part-time course fee income exceeds budget.		
The faculty should continue to cover the full-time vacancy with part-time staff as the savings made from the full-time salaries budget are more than twice the additional amount spent in part-time salaries.		
Total actual income is less than the total budgeted income, but total actual expenditure is greater than the total budgeted expenditure.		
The faculty should investigate why the numbers of students registering for part-time courses was less than expected.		
The faculty should increase marketing activity to promote higher numbers of students registering for the one-day practical bookkeeping course and the revision courses.		
The reduced numbers of students registering for full-time and one-day courses has led to a reduction in expenditure on registration fees.		

(ii) **Select which of the following would be the most suitable title for this report:**

	✓
Business and finance budget	
Faculty income and expenditure performance review	
Faculty income and expenditure results	
Review of business and finance faculty income and expenditure against budget	
Review of business and finance	

(b) **Identify which ONE of the following describes the contents of the 'main body' section of a business report.**

	✓
Provides suggested actions to overcome the problems identified	
Provides an analysis of the results of the research	
Summarises the main points of the research and analysis	
Provides suggested actions to be taken in the future	

(c) **Complete the following statement by selecting the most appropriate answer from the picklist.**

When considering the order of a formal business report, which section will usually appear between the executive summary and the main body?

Picklist:

Appendices
Conclusions
Introduction
Title

Task 64

You work in the accounts department and have been asked by your Manager, Nigel Allen, to send a memo to David Wright, a manager in the sales department. You know David well as you often provide him with financial analysis. Nigel wants you to let David know that the accounting department needs to receive all sales department expense claims relating to expenses in May 20X2 by 10 June 20X2. This is so that all sales department staff can be reimbursed for their May expenses before the end of June 20X2. Today's date is 1 June 20X2.

Complete the memo below. Select the appropriate items from the picklist.

MEMO

From: AAT student

To: **(1)** [▼]

Date: **(2)** [▼]

Subject: **(3)** [▼]

(4) [▼] , accounts department manager, has asked me to inform you

that this month, all sales department expense claims relating to **(5)** [▼]

expenses must be passed to the accounting department by **(6)** [▼] at

the latest.

This is so that we can ensure all **(7)** [▼] employees are reimbursed

before the end of **(8)** [▼] .

Thanks

AAT student

Picklist:

(1)   David Write / Nigel Allen / David Right / Nigel Alan / David Wright
(2)   31 May 20X2 / 1 June 20X2 / 10 June 20X2 / 30 June 20X2
(3)   Providing financial analysis / Expense claim deadline / Meeting notification
(4)   David Write / Nigel Allen / David Right / Nigel Alan / David Wright
(5)   May 20X2 / June 20X2 / July 20X2
(6)   31 May 20X2 / 1 June 20X2 / 10 June 20X2 / 30 June 20X2
(7)   sales department / accounting department
(8)   May 20X2 / June 20X2 / July 20X2

Task 65

You are helping to prepare a report to present the findings of a recent project commissioned to establish how effectively key internal controls are operating within the business and within individual departments. Internal controls are processes that help to make sure the organisation or an area of the business meets its objectives, so it is important they are working properly (operating effectively). The findings from the project have been summarised below:

Department	Number of key controls identified	Number of key controls tested	Number of key controls found to be operating effectively
Accounting	20	18	10
Personnel	12	10	6
Purchasing	14	12	7
Sales	16	10	7

(a) **In which section of the report is the table above most likely to appear?**

	✓
Executive Summary	
Introduction	
Appendix	
Recommendations Section	

(b) **Which THREE of the following are valid conclusions for the report?**

	✓
The majority of the key controls tested are operating effectively.	
The majority of the key controls identified are operating effectively.	
The majority of the key controls identified were tested.	
Based on the key controls tested, the sales department had the highest percentage of key controls operating effectively.	
Based on the key controls identified, the purchasing department had the highest percentage of its key controls tested.	
The same number of key controls were tested in the purchasing department as in the sales department.	

(c) **Complete the following sentence to give a valid recommendation for inclusion in the report.**

There should be an investigation into

Picklist:

how the ineffective key controls can be modified to ensure they operate effectively.

why the accounting department has more key controls than each of the other departments.

Task 66

What would be the most appropriate method of communication in each of the following circumstances? Choose from the picklist below.

(a) Explaining to a customer that a prompt payment discount that has been deducted was not valid, as the invoice was not paid within the discount period

(b) Requesting customer balances from a colleague in the sales ledger department

(c) Providing negative feedback to a colleague on the quality of their work

(d) A formal complaint to a supplier regarding the delivery times of goods, which are not as agreed

(e) Information to be provided to the sales director regarding the breakdown of sales geographically for the last two years

Picklist:

Email
Face to face discussion
Letter
Telephone

Task 67

A junior colleague shows you a draft of an email to the Purchasing Director of a company which has recently expressed an interest in your products. He asks you to identify any words or phrases you think are inappropriate. The draft appears as follows.

To:	hgwells@retail.com
From:	acdoyle@southfield.co.uk
Date:	[Today's date]
Subject:	Your recent enquiry
Attach:	Sales brochure.pdf

Hi, Hugh.

Thanks for your msg re our products. Its cool that you were able to come and see our display at the Home Entertainment Trade Fair. More than happy to help with further info.

Our company's one of the best in the field, and our product's have recently one an award as Retail Product of the Year.

I've attached a brochure what details our full product range. it includes prices and terms of trade. Having received it, I will contact you to see if you'd like to place an order.

In the meantime, me and the sales team are availble to answer any questions you may have, it'd be gr8 to hear from you.

Cheers.

Arthur

(a) **Underline any inappropriate words or phrases in the email.**

(b) **Re-draft the email and make a note of how you would explain your changes to Arthur, to help him improve his communication skills.**

Task 68

The business you work for ordered five laptop computers with a list price of £500 each (order ref NCA124). During a phone conversation on 1 May 20X1 you were promised a 5% bulk discount by an account manager at the supplier (Bell computers) if you purchased five or more laptops. The Account Manager at the supplier is called Bill Fences.

The laptops arrived today (20 May 20X1) and so did the invoice from the supplier (Invoice number LT241). The invoice shows the total value of the computers to be £2,500 and the 5% discount had not been deducted. You have tried phoning Bill but he is out of the office today.

You are on holiday for the rest of the week and are not going to be able to deal with this so your supervisor Hugh Martin has asked you to send him a short memo explaining what happened with any photocopies of related documents attached. He will then contact the supplier to ask for a credit note and a new invoice.

Complete the memo below by selecting the appropriate option from the appropriate picklist, or entering the appropriate reference or number. A drop-down icon indicates there is a picklist available and each picklist is numbered. (If there is no drop-down icon you must simply enter the reference/number.)

MEMO

To: (1) [▾]

From: Anne Accountant, Accountant

Date: (2) [▾]

Subject: Bell computers: **(3)** [▾] for laptops.

On **(4)** [▾] an order (reference [   ]) was placed for five laptop computers which have a list price of £ [   ] each. On the same day **(5)** [▾], an account manager at Bell, agreed we would receive a 5% bulk discount because the order was for five or more computers. I enclose my notes from the phone call (including contact details for the account manager) and a copy of the order for your information.

We received invoice (reference [   ]) for the computers today which shows the total cost of the laptops to be £ [   ]. Therefore the anticipated discount of £ [   ] has not been applied and we should request that Bell send us a credit note for the original invoice and re-issue a new invoice with the discount applied.

Many thanks for dealing with this.

Anne

Enc: Copies of the order and invoice
Notes of phone call on 1 May 20X1

Picklist:

(1)   Hugh Martin, Accounts Supervisor / Bill Fences, Account Manager
(2)   1 May 20X1 / 20 May 20X1 / 31 May 20X1
(3)   Undercharge / Overcharge
(4)   1 May 20X1 / 20 May 20X1 / 31 May 20X1
(5)   Hugh Martin / Bill Fences

Task 69

A new project is to be started at your workplace and your manager is assembling a team to work on it. Some of your colleagues are not used to working in teams.

Write a brief report to be distributed to staff explaining what team working is and setting out the benefits.

Task 70

A number of issues have arisen in your workplace because of missed deadlines. Your manager has asked you to draft an email to be sent to all staff explaining the importance of deadlines and how to deal with problems in meeting deadlines.

Insert your text in this box.

To: staff@anycompany.com
From: aatstudent@anycompany.com
Subject: Deadlines

Task 71

For which ONE of the following could a spreadsheet be used?

	✓
Maintaining detailed customer records	
Preparing budgets and forecasts	
Sending out supplier statements	

Task 72

Which THREE of the following are true regarding spreadsheets?

	✓
Spreadsheets are used to store and manipulate data.	
Spreadsheets can be used for word processing.	
Data in a spreadsheet can be easily updated.	
Spreadsheet data can be output in the form of graphs.	
Spreadsheets can be used to replace accounting packages.	
Sophisticated databases are making spreadsheets obsolete.	

Answer Bank

Answer bank

Assessment objective 1 – Work Effectively in Finance

Task 1

(a)

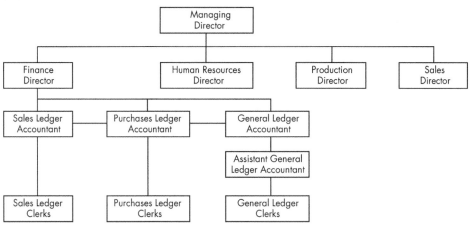

(b)

Action	✓
Maximise inventory levels	
Issue statements to trade receivables on a regular basis	✓
Pay trade payables as soon as invoices are received	
Encourage trade receivables to pay the amounts owed on or before the due date	✓
Ensure the organisation has a staff development policy	
Issue statements to trade payables on a regular basis	

Task 2

(a)

Action	✓
Complete the additional task as your manager is the most senior person you work for and do whatever other work you can. The colleague will have to wait for their work until you have time to complete it.	
Complete the additional task as your manager is the most senior person you work for and do whatever other work you can. You will prioritise the colleague's work for the next day.	
Complete the colleague's work as they asked you to do the work first and you will start the manager's work tomorrow.	
Discuss your workload with both the manager and the colleague to decide on the work priority and renegotiate deadlines where appropriate.	✓

(b)

Statement	True ✓	False ✓
There will be no impact. If you can't check supplier statements on Thursday, you can prioritise this work the next day.		✓
Your colleague may be unable to pay suppliers by the due date which may result in problems for the organisation in receiving future supplies.	✓	

(c)

Team effectiveness
All team members have clearly defined objectives and responsibilities
Each team member is willing and able to cover the work of other team members if necessary
Good communication within the team

Task 3

(a)

	✓
Arrange virtual rather than face to face team meetings	✓
Have all office lighting linked to motion sensors so they automatically switch off when the office is empty	✓
Always select the lowest priced suppliers of goods and services	
Ensure all trainee accountants complete CPD	
Do business only with organisations which can demonstrate they follow responsible environmental practices	✓
Ensure costs and expenses are minimised in every instance	
Arrange monthly management meetings at a central point in the country rather than at head office	
Restrict paper usage to the printing of essential documents only	✓

(b)

Statement	True ✓	False ✓
Sustainability means ensuring the organisation focuses purely on generating the highest profit irrespective of the consequences of the organisation's actions.		✓
When building new premises, trying to ensure the building is carbon neutral even if this results in increased initial costs is an example of a sustainable initiative by the organisation.	✓	
Sustainable initiatives do not apply to those in an accounting function but such initiatives do apply to the production function.		✓
Having a policy of office buildings being well insulated and solar powered may help to reduce the running costs of the organisation and also have a positive effect on the environment.	✓	

Task 4

(a)

	✓
Company vehicle servicing policy	
Sales visit procedures	
Expenses payment procedures	✓
Production shift handover procedures	

(b)

	✓
The accounting function has a legal obligation to review the credit policy every two years.	
Organisational procedures prevent staff from suggesting improvements to work processes.	
It is good practice for organisations to explain the fire evacuation procedures during staff induction training.	✓
The Staff Development policy only applies to those working in the human resources department.	
Many organisational policies and procedures are designed to ensure that working practices comply with legal requirements.	✓
The Data Protection policy is an example of a policy that would not apply to those staff working in an accounting function.	

Task 5

Monday To-do list	Tuesday To-do list	Time
Closing stock breakdown	Accounting function meeting	09:00–10:00
Closing stock breakdown	Region 6 expenses analysis	10:00–11:00
Regional reconciliation	Region 6 expenses analysis	11:00–12:00
Wages analysis	Petty cash top up	12:00–13:00

Task 6

(a)

Accounting trainee's development activities
Sit with a colleague when the monthly budget reports are produced
Read a book on standard costing in a production environment

(b)

Consequences of NOT maintaining CPD activities
If knowledge is not up to date then staff could give incorrect professional advice.
A chartered accountant may be prevented from continuing as a member of their professional body.

(c)

Statement	True ✓	False ✓
Conducting research in the library at the local college as part of your AAT studies is one type of CPD activity.	✓	
Making sure that an accounting trainee has completed sufficient CPD activities is the sole responsibility of the organisation's Human Resources department.		✓

Task 7

(a)

Situation	Fundamental ethical principle applicable
You are asked by a colleague to provide the contact details of a client as they were at school together.	Confidentiality
You have been asked to complete a VAT return which is a subject you have not yet studied at college and about which you have little knowledge.	Professional Competence
Your organisation has a Disciplinary and Grievance policy which applies to all staff in the organisation from the most senior partner down.	Professional Behaviour
A new accountant asks you to check an advertisement which is to be placed in the local newspaper. In this he states 'We are the best accountants in the area and half the price of Jones and Co'.	Professional Behaviour

(b) **(i)** Whilst conducting a year-end audit at a client's business the client offers to take you on an all-expenses paid holiday to her villa in Spain once you have finished the year-end work.

	✓
Politely decline the offer and do not tell anyone about it.	
Politely accept the offer but ask the client not to mention the holiday to any other members of the audit team.	
Politely accept the offer and work extremely hard to finish the year-end work.	
Politely decline the offer and discuss the situation with your manager.	✓

(ii) You have been asked to act as an interviewer to help assess and select prospective new trainees for your organisation. Your niece has been selected for one of the interviews.

	✓
Complete the work as interviewer but treat each interviewee fairly and don't tell anyone about your connection with one of the applicants.	
Complete the work as interviewer and ensure you are able to help your niece through to the next stage of the recruitment process.	
Refuse to be involved in any aspect of the assessment and selection of prospective trainees but do not explain to your manager why.	
Discuss the situation with your manager to see if you could complete the work but abstain from being involved in the assessment of your niece.	✓

(iii) You have been asked by a family friend to advise them of the names of current bidders and details of their offers regarding a contract that they wish to tender for.

	✓
Provide them with the requested details of current bidders and their offers.	
Provide them with the requested details of the names of the bidders but not the details of their offers.	
Politely decline to provide any details explaining you are not allowed to disclose such information.	✓
Provide them with incorrect details of the other bidders' offers.	

(c)

Sometimes, but only if you have the permission of the client.

Task 8

(a) This policy has been compiled to aid compliance with Data Protection Legislation.

(b)

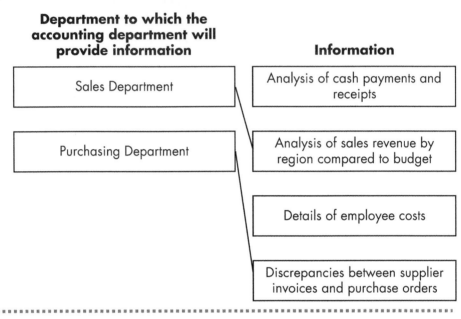

Department to which the accounting department will provide information	**Information**
Sales Department	Analysis of cash payments and receipts
Purchasing Department	Analysis of sales revenue by region compared to budget
	Details of employee costs
	Discrepancies between supplier invoices and purchase orders

Task 9

Action	Contributes to
Reduce customer credit terms so they pay their debts earlier	The management of working capital and solvency
Ensure IT support is in place in case staff encounter computer problems	The smooth running of the business
Produce a Health and Safety policy to be circulated to all staff	Compliance with applicable laws and regulations
Ensure all staff are paid at least the minimum wage	Compliance with applicable laws and regulations
Ensure staff recruited for each job have the relevant experience and skills	The smooth running of the business
Avoid the build-up of surplus inventories	The management of working capital and solvency

Task 10

(a) An $\boxed{\text{organisation chart}}$ is used to show the structure of an organisation or function.

(b)

	✓
Jill reports to Bill	
James reports to Jill	
Nicky reports to Bill	
Nicky reports to Jill	✓
Bill reports to James	✓
Emily reports to Jill	

(c)

Issue	Resolve myself ✓	Refer to line manager ✓
Your line manager has asked you to complete a calculation of wage deductions. However, having started to look at the calculation, it is more complex than you thought and you do not feel you have had enough training to be able to perform it.		✓
You suspect a colleague has been setting up fictitious employees on the payroll in order to commit fraud.		✓
Your colleague has asked you to swap your work for the afternoon with her work, as yours looks more 'exciting'. However, you do not know how to carry out her tasks.	✓	
You feel you are being bullied by a colleague.		✓

Task 11

	✓
Produce a cash budget	✓
Produce a profit statement	
Ensure tax bills are paid on time	
Ensure inventory is kept at maximum levels	
Ensure receivables pay on time	✓
Monitor the cash budget	✓

Task 12

Order	Task
1st task (10:00am to 12:00pm)	Enter sales invoices/credit notes into computer system
2nd task (12:00pm to 1:00pm)	Enter weekly purchase invoices into the computer
3rd task (2:00pm to 4:00pm) (20 × 6 mins = 120 mins)	Match purchase invoices to goods received notes and pass to the accountant for authorisation
4th task (4:00pm to 5:00pm)	Filing

Task 13

Daily tasks	Enter sales invoices into the computer Enter cash/cheque receipts into the computer Enter cash/cheque payments into computer Deal with petty cash claims
Weekly tasks	Enter petty cash details into the computer Assist in preparation of payroll
Monthly tasks	Prepare bank reconciliation

Unallocated: Other ad hoc accounting tasks.

Task 14

(a) | Independence | is NOT an advantage of working in a team rather than as an individual.

(b) The correct answer is: Assertive

If you are trying to influence someone, you will need to communicate assertively (without being aggressive) and put forward your views clearly. You will need to listen, first, to the other person, so that you can argue logically against their reasons, and can tailor your solution to their needs.

Task 15

Description	Element of SMART
Objectives must be achievable using available time and other resources	Realistic
Objectives must be formulated such that the achievement of them can be evaluated	Measurable
Objectives must be set within a specific timescale	Time-bounded
Development objectives must not be general	Specific
Must be approved by the appropriate manager	Agreed

Task 16

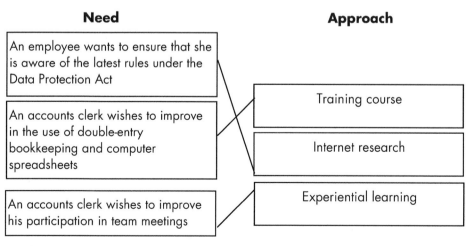

Task 17

	✓
Failure to keep up to date on CPD	
A personal financial interest in the client's affairs	✓
Being negligent or reckless with the accuracy of the information provided to the client	

A personal financial interest in the client's affairs will affect objectivity. Failure to keep up to date on CPD is an issue of professional competence, while providing inaccurate information reflects upon professional integrity.

Task 18

Apply safeguards to eliminate or reduce the threat to an acceptable level	3
Evaluate the seriousness of the threat	2
Discontinue the action or relationship giving rise to the threat	4
Identify a potential threat to a fundamental ethical principle	1

Assessment objective 2 – Bookkeeping Transactions

Task 19

(a) Cash book – credit side

Details	Cash £	Bank £	VAT £	Trade payables £	Cash purchases £
Balance b/f		2,312			
Mendip plc	378		63		315
Landa Ltd		1,950		1,950	
Bebe and Co		726		726	
Total	378	4,988	63	2,676	315

(b) **Working:** £200 + £319 – £378

£141

(c) **Working:** £1,964 – £4,988

–£3,024

Task 20

(a) General ledger

Account name	Amount £	Debit	Credit
VAT	265	✓	
Purchases ledger control account	10,900	✓	
Cash purchases	1,325	✓	
Bank charges	48	✓	

(b) Purchases ledger

Account name	Amount £	Debit	Credit
D B Franks	264	✓	

Task 21

Trial balance as at 30 June

Account name	Amount £	Debit £	Credit £
Miscellaneous expenses	2,116	2,116	
Bank interest received	199		199
Bank interest paid	342	342	
Petty cash control	175	175	
Office expenses	3,793	3,793	
Motor expenses	1,118	1,118	
Loan from bank	15,000		15,000
Rent and rates	3,000	3,000	
Motor vehicles	37,650	37,650	
Sales	198,575		198,575
Purchases returns	875		875
Sales ledger control	128,331	128,331	
Bank (overdraft)	2,246		2,246
Purchases ledger control	55,231		55,231
VAT (owing to HM Revenue & Customs)	4,289		4,289
Wages	37,466	37,466	
Purchases	88,172	88,172	
Capital	25,748		25,748
Totals		302,163	302,163

Task 22

(a)–(c)

J B Mills

Date 20XX	Details	Amount £	Date 20XX	Details	Amount £
1 Jun	Balance b/f	1,585	22 Jun	Bank	678
11 Jun	Invoice 1269	1,804	29 Jun	Credit note 049	607
			30 Jun	Balance c/d	2,104
	Total	3,389		Total	3,389
1 Jul	Balance b/d	2,104			

Task 23

(a)

Assets £	Liabilities £	Capital £
35,720	10,000	25,720

(b)

Assets £	Liabilities £	Capital £
43,463	11,270	32,193

(c)

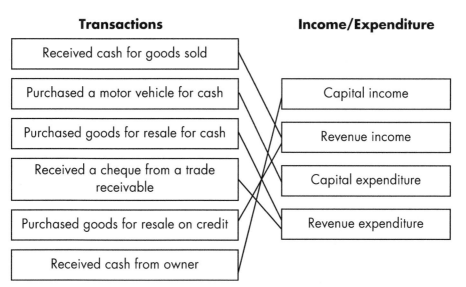

(d)   The correct answer is: No

(e)

Customer name	Customer account code
Avion Ltd	AVI01
Blakely plc	BLA01
Brandon and Co	BRA02
Fellows Designs	FEL01
Nailer and Co	NAI01
MBJ Ltd	MBJ01
Patel Products	PAT01
Pound plc	POU02
Pickford Ltd	PIC03
Portman and Co	POR04
TJK Ltd	TJK01

Task 24

	Cash transaction ✓	Credit transaction ✓
Purchase of goods for £500 payable by cash in one week's time		✓
Arranging a bank draft for the purchase of a new computer	✓	
Sale of goods to a customer on account		✓
Sale of goods to a customer who paid by credit card at time of transaction	✓	
Purchase of goods where payment is due in three week's time		✓

Task 25

Goods total £	Trade discount (15% × price) £	Net total £
542.60	81.39	461.21
107.50	16.13	91.37
98.40	14.76	83.64
257.10	38.57	218.53
375.00	56.25	318.75

Task 26

Net total £	VAT (Net × 20%) £	Gross total £
236.40	47.28	283.68
372.10	74.42	446.52
85.60	17.12	102.72
159.40	31.88	191.28
465.30	93.06	558.36

Task 27

Gross total £	VAT (Invoice total × 20/120) £	Net total £
277.24	46.21	231.03
163.42	27.24	136.18
49.74	8.29	41.45
108.28	18.05	90.23
69.42	11.57	57.85
831.20	138.53	692.67

Task 28

(a)–(b) Sales day book

Customer	Invoice number	Total £	VAT £	Net £
Watsons Ltd	7541	656.40	109.40	547.00
Harrison	7542	792.00	132.00	660.00
Valu Shopping	7543	415.20	69.20	346.00
Fishers	7544	393.60	65.60	328.00
Harrison	7545	657.60	109.60	548.00
Villa Discount	7546	169.20	28.20	141.00
Valu Shopping	7547	499.20	83.20	416.00
Watsons Ltd	7548	285.60	47.60	238.00
Fishers	7549	366.00	61.00	305.00
		4,234.80	705.80	3,529.00

Cross-cast check:

	£
Net	3,529.00
VAT	705.80
Total	4,234.80

Task 29

Purchases day book

Date 20XX	Details	Invoice number	Total £	VAT £	Net £
30 June	Bramley Ltd	7623	3,085.20	514.20	2,571.00
30 June	Russett & Co	0517	2,400.00	400.00	2,000.00
	Totals		5,485.20	914.20	4,571.00

Purchases ledger

Account name	Amount £	Debit ✓	Credit ✓
Bramley Ltd	3,085.20		✓
Russett & Co	2,400.00		✓

Task 30

	✓
You have requested a credit note from the supplier for £1,586 which you have not yet received.	
You sent a cheque for £1,586 to the supplier on 30 June 20XX.	✓
You ordered some items from the supplier on 30 June for £1,586 but the goods have not yet been delivered and an invoice has not yet been raised.	

Task 31

Matilda's Machinery
1 North Street
Westbury, WE11 9SD

To: Frampton Ltd   Date: 31 October 20XX

Date 20XX	Details	Transaction amount £	Outstanding amount £
15 September	Invoice 1540	656	656
29 September	Invoice 1560	742	1,398
3 October	Credit note 89	43	1,355
10 October	Invoice 1580	1,235	2,590
15 October	Cheque	682	1,908

Task 32

(a) The correct answer is: £21

Working:

	£
Opening balance	27
Cash from bank	48
Less: expenditure during month	(21)
balance at end of month	54

Therefore 75 – 54 = £21 required to restore the imprest level

(b) The correct answer is: Debit

Assessment objective 3 – Bookkeeping Controls/Elements of Costing

Task 33

The Journal

Account name	Amount £	Debit ✓	Credit ✓
Capital	4,780		✓
Office expenses	1,927	✓	
Sales	8,925		✓
Purchases	4,212	✓	
Commission received	75		✓
Discounts received	54		✓
Cash at bank	1,814	✓	
Petty cash	180	✓	
Loan from bank	5,000		✓
Motor expenses	372	✓	
Motor vehicles	9,443	✓	
Other expenses	886	✓	
Journal to record opening entries of new business.			

Task 34

(a)

Account name	Amount £	Debit ✓	Credit ✓
Bank	12,565	✓	
Computer equipment	12,565		✓

(b)

Account name	Amount £	Debit ✓	Credit ✓
Computer equipment	12,265	✓	
Bank	12,265		✓

Task 35

Commission received

Details	Amount £	Details	Amount £
Rent received	545		

Rent received

Details	Amount £	Details	Amount £
		Commission received	545

Suspense

Details	Amount £	Details	Amount £
Balance b/f	2,682	General repairs	3,667
Legal fees	985		

Legal fees

Details	Amount £	Details	Amount £
		Suspense	985

General repairs

Details	Amount £	Details	Amount £
Suspense	3,667		

Task 36

Trial balance

Account names	Balances extracted on 30 June £	Debit balances at 1 July £	Credit balances at 1 July £
Capital	20,774		20,774
Motor vehicles	47,115	47,115	
Cash at bank	11,923	12,735	
Cash	200	1,012	
Sales ledger control	120,542	120,542	
Purchases ledger control	60,224		60,224
VAT (owing to HM Revenue and Customs)	7,916		7,916
Office expenses	3,216	3,216	
Sales	207,426		207,757
Purchases	99,250	98,919	
Motor expenses	4,310	4,310	
Other expenses	8,822	8,822	
Totals		296,671	296,671

Task 37

Tutorial note. Cheque 001499 for £1,015 on the bank statement was taken into account in the previous bank reconciliation, since the difference between the opening balance on the bank statement and the cash book is £5,119 – £4,104 = £1,015. Therefore it should not appear on the bank reconciliation.

Bank reconciliation statement as at 30 September 20XX	£
Balance as per bank statement	37,466
Add:	
Kington Ltd	3,970
Total to add	3,970
Less:	
Newton West	195
Welland Ltd	234
Roman plc	316
Total to subtract	745
Balance as per cash book	40,691

Task 38

(a) Sales ledger control account

Details	Amount £	Debit ✓	Credit ✓
Balance owing from credit customers at 1 July	101,912	✓	
Money received from credit customers	80,435		✓
Irrecoverable debts	228		✓
Goods sold to credit customers	70,419	✓	
Goods returned by credit customers	2,237		✓

(b) Purchases ledger control account

Details	Amount £	Debit ✓	Credit ✓
Balance owing to credit suppliers at 1 July	61,926		✓
Journal debit to correct an error	550	✓	
Goods returned to credit suppliers	1,128	✓	
Purchases from credit suppliers	40,525		✓
Payments made to credit suppliers	45,763	✓	

(c)

Balance	✓
Credit balance b/d on 1 September of £65,050	
Debit balance b/d on 1 September of £65,050	✓
Credit balance b/d on 1 September of £67,500	
Debit balance b/d on 1 September of £67,500	

(d)

Statements	True ✓	False ✓
The purchases ledger control account enables a business to identify how much is owing to credit suppliers in total.	✓	
The total of the balances in the purchases ledger should reconcile with the balance of the sales ledger control account.		✓

Task 39

(a)   VAT control

Details	Amount £	Details	Amount £
Balance b/f – owing from HMRC	13,146	Sales	31,197
Purchases	19,220	Purchases returns	2,465
Sales returns	1,779	Cash sales	1,910
Petty cash	98	VAT refund	7,131
Irrecoverable debts	950	Office equipment sold	200

(b) Tutorial note. The balance is a £7,710 credit balance. That is the amount owed to HMRC.

	✓
Yes	
No	✓

(c)

	✓
The VAT control account is used to record the VAT amount of transactions and to help prepare the VAT return.	✓
The VAT control account is used to record the VAT amount of transactions but has no connection with the VAT return.	

Task 40

(a)

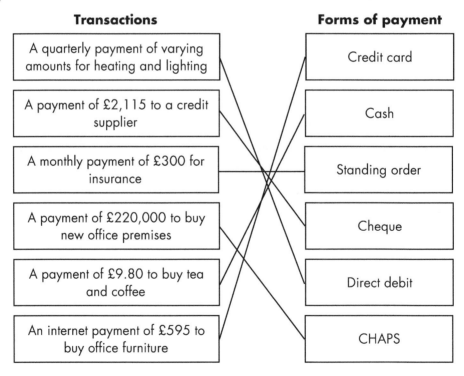

Transactions	Forms of payment
A quarterly payment of varying amounts for heating and lighting	Credit card
A payment of £2,115 to a credit supplier	Cash
A monthly payment of £300 for insurance	Standing order
A payment of £220,000 to buy new office premises	Cheque
A payment of £9.80 to buy tea and coffee	Direct debit
An internet payment of £595 to buy office furniture	CHAPS

(b)

Statements	True ✓	False ✓
Purchases made using a debit card will result in funds being immediately transferred from Gold's bank account.	✓	
Before accepting a payment by cheque from a new customer, Gold should ask the bank if there are sufficient funds in the customer's bank account.		✓

Task 41

Transaction	Payment out ✓	Payment in ✓
£725 paid into the bank		✓
Direct debit of £47	✓	
Cheque payment of £124.60	✓	
Interest charged on the overdraft	✓	
BACS payment for wages	✓	

Task 42

(a)

Cash book

Date	Details	Bank £	Date	Cheque no.	Details	Bank £
01 Nov	Balance b/f	6,775	03 Nov	110870	Robots & Co	5,175
24 Nov	Bishops Ltd	1,822	03 Nov	110871	W Bevan	1,234
24 Nov	Griplock Ltd	7,998	06 Nov	110872	Fishhooks Ltd	2,250
21 Nov	BBT Ltd	8,000	10 Nov	110873	Sanding Supplies	275
24 Nov	Welders Ltd	2,555	17 Nov	110874	Waders & Co	76
			21 Nov	Direct debit	Insurance	500

Date	Details	Bank £	Date	Cheque no.	Details	Bank £
			24 Nov	Direct debit	Chainsaw Ltd	88
			30 Nov		Balance c/d	17,552
		27,150				27,150
1 Dec	Balance b/d	17,552				

Note. Cheque number 110865 on the bank statement: the first cheque in the cash book in November is number 110870. As the difference between the opening balances on the bank statement and in the cash book is for the amount of this cheque (£2,361) it is reasonable to assume that cheque 110865 was entered in the cash book in a previous month and would have been a reconciling item in the bank reconciliation in the previous month. This cheque should be ticked to the October bank reconciliation.

(b)

Bank reconciliation statement as at 30 November	£	£
Balance per bank statement:		8,083
Add:		
Bishops Ltd	1,822	
Griplock Ltd	7,998	
Total to add		9,820
Less:		
Sanding Supplies	275	
Waders & Co	76	
Total to subtract		351
Balance as per cash book		17,552

Task 43

Sales ledger control

Details	£	Details	£
Balance b/f	27,321	Sales returns	1,934
Sales	11,267	Bank	10,006
		Irrecoverable debts	742
		Balance c/d	25,906
	38,588		38,588

Task 44

Purchases ledger control

Details	£	Details	£
Purchases returns	751	Balance b/f	6,547
Bank	8,653	Purchases	9,317
Discounts received	481		
Balance c/d	5,979		
	15,864		15,864

Task 45

	Control account ✓	List of balances ✓	Both ✓
Invoice entered into the sales day book as £540 instead of £450			✓
Purchases day book overcast by £1,100	✓		
An invoice taken as £430 instead of £330 when being posted to the customer's account		✓	
Incorrect balancing of a memorandum ledger account		✓	
A purchases return not entered into the purchases returns day book			✓

Task 46

Sales ledger control

Details	£	Details	£
Balance b/f	12,467	(i) Sales returns	100
		(iii) Irrecoverable debts	250
		Balance c/d	12,117
	12,467		12,467
Balance b/d	12,117		

	£
Sales ledger list of balances	11,858
Error: (ii) Over-statement of receipt (430 – 340)	90
Error: (iv) Balance omitted	169
Amended list of balances	12,117
Amended control account balance	12,117

Task 47

Journal

Account name	Amount £	Debit ✓	Credit ✓
Capital	20,000		✓
Furniture and fittings	5,315	✓	
Sales	107,318		✓
Motor vehicles	10,109	✓	
Cash at bank	15,000	✓	
Purchases	96,120	✓	
Sales returns	750	✓	
Purchases ledger control	27,238		✓
Sales ledger control	51,759	✓	
Loan from bank	17,000		✓
Motor expenses	1,213	✓	
VAT	8,710		✓

Task 48

(a)

Cost	Material ✓	Labour ✓	Overhead ✓
Insurance of office computers			✓
Ink cartridges used in the production of pens	✓		
Wages of employees in the production department		✓	
Card used to produce binders for notebooks	✓		

(b)

Cost	Direct ✓	Indirect ✓
Insurance of factory		✓
Paper used in the manufacture of envelopes	✓	
Salary of production manager		✓
Plastic used in the production of pens	✓	

Task 49

(a)

Cost	Production ✓	Administration ✓	Selling and distribution ✓	Finance ✓
Fruit purchased for use in drinks	✓			
Stationery provided to all departments		✓		
Interest charged on bank loan				✓
Sales campaign			✓	

(b)

Cost	Fixed ✓	Variable ✓	Semi-variable ✓
Employees in the bottling department paid on a piecework basis		✓	
Annual consultancy charge for updating the website	✓		
Sugar used in drinks		✓	
Machinery hire consisting of a fixed rental charge and a usage charge			✓

Task 50

Profit/Cost centre	Cost code	Sub-classification	Sub-code	Transaction	Code
Sales	120	Sportswear	075		
		Leisurewear	085		
Production	230	Direct cost	160	Sales of football shirts	120/075
		Indirect cost	170	Cotton used in leisure shirts	230/160
Administration	340	Direct cost	255	Cleaning materials used in factory	230/170
		Indirect cost	265	Sales of casual shorts	120/085
Selling and Distribution	450	Direct cost	340	Heating of administration offices	340/265
		Indirect cost	350	Cost of advertising campaign	450/350

Task 51

Activity	Code	Nature of cost	Sub-code	Transaction	Code
Investments	IN	External	210	External funds used to set up investment	IN210
		Internal	240	External contractor charge	CO640
Revenues	RE	UK	320	Material used on project	CO420
		Overseas	350	Salaries paid to employees	CO530
Costs	CO	Material	420	Project revenue arising in the UK	RE320
		Labour	530	Firstglow Ltd company funds invested in project	IN240
		Overheads	640		

Task 52

(a)

Cost	Yes ✓	No ✓
Fee paid to an external accountant	✓	
Salary of chief executive	✓	
Wages of production workers making the product		✓

(b) **Unit product cost at the production level of 75,000 units.**

Element	Unit Product Cost £
Materials	22
Labour	12
Direct Cost	34
Overheads	26
Total	60

Workings:

Materials: (50,000 × £33)/75,000 = £22 per unit of product

Labour: (40,000 × £22.50)/75,000 = £12 per unit of product

Overheads: £1,950,000/75,000 = £26 per unit

Task 53

(a)

Costs	£	Manufacturing account	£
Manufacturing cost		Opening inventory of raw materials	52,700
Direct labour	144,000	Purchase of raw materials	221,100
Cost of goods sold		Closing inventory of raw materials	48,100
Cost of goods manufactured		**Direct materials used**	
Closing inventory of finished goods	101,200	Direct labour	144,000
Direct cost		**Direct cost**	
Opening inventory of raw materials	52,700	Manufacturing overheads	237,400

Costs	£	Manufacturing account	£
Closing inventory of raw materials	48,100	**Manufacturing cost**	
Closing inventory of work in progress	74,200	Opening inventory of work in progress	72,400
Manufacturing overheads	237,400	Closing inventory of work in progress	74,200
Direct materials used		**Cost of goods manufactured**	
Opening inventory of finished goods	107,600	Opening inventory of finished goods	107,600
Opening inventory of work in progress	72,400	Closing inventory of finished goods	101,200
Purchase of raw materials	221,100	**Cost of goods sold**	

(b)

Manufacturing account	£
Direct materials used	225,700
Direct cost	369,700
Manufacturing cost	607,100
Cost of goods manufactured	605,300
Cost of goods sold	611,700

Task 54

(a)

Statement	FIFO ✓	LIFO ✓	AVCO ✓
The closing inventory is valued at £4,800	✓		
The issue of 2,400 units is costed at £17,280			✓
The issue of 2,400 units is costed at £18,000		✓	

(b)

Statement	True ✓	False ✓
AVCO values the closing inventory at £4,320	✓	
FIFO costs the issue of 2,400 units at £16,900		✓
LIFO values the closing inventory at £3,600	✓	

Workings:

	Units	Per unit £	Total £	Balance £
Opening inventory	1,200	6	7,200	7,200
Received	1,800	8	14,400	21,600
	3,000			
Issued	(2,400)			
Closing inventory	600			

	FIFO	LIFO	AVCO
Issue	(1,200 × £6) + (1,200 × £8) = £16,800	(600 × £6) + (1,800 × £8) = £18,000	2,400 × £21,600/3,000 = £17,280
Closing inventory	600 × £8 = £4,800	600 × £6 = £3,600	600 × £21,600/3,000 = £4,320

Task 55

Method	Cost of issue on 19 February £	Closing inventory at 28 February £
FIFO	9,800	19,400
LIFO	11,500	17,700
AVCO	10,500	18,700

Workings:

	Units	Per unit £	Total £	Balance £
4 Feb Receipt	1,000	4	4,000	4,000
7 Feb Receipt	500	5	2,500	6,500
11 Feb Receipt	2,000	5.50	11,000	17,500
	3,500			
19 Feb Issue	(2,100)			
	1,400			
24 Feb Receipt	1,800	6.50	11,700	
24 Feb Closing inventory	3,200			

	FIFO	LIFO	AVCO
Issue	(1,000 × £4) + (500 × £5) + (600 × £5.50) = £9,800	(2,000 × £5.50) + (100 × £5) = £11,500	2,100 × £17,500/3,500 = £10,500
Closing inventory	(1,400 × £5.50) + £11,700 = £19,400	(1,000 × £4) + (400 × £5) + £11,700 = £17,700	£17,500 – £10,500 + £11,700 = £18,700

Task 56

(a)

Statements	True ✓	False ✓
During a 36 hour week an employee produces 910 units and does not receive a bonus (W1)		✓
During a 40 hour week an employee produces 1,180 units and receives a bonus of £36 (W2)	✓	
During a 37 hour week an employee produces 980 units and receives total pay of £307 (W3)	✓	

Workings:

1 Expected output: 36 × 25 = 900 units. Producing 910 items means the employee DOES receive a bonus

2 Expected output: 40 × 25 = 1,000 units, producing 180 extra units results in a bonus of 180 × £0.20 = £36

3 Expected output: 37 × 25 = 925 units. Total pay: (37 × £8) + ((980 − 925) × £0.20) = £307

(b)

Employee	Hours worked	Basic wage £	Overtime £	Gross wage £
V. Chopra	40	450.00	60.00	510.00
R. Silvai	43	450.00	105.00	555.00

Workings:

	Basic £	Overtime £
V. Chopra	36 × £12.50	4 × £15.00
R. Silvai	36 × £12.50	7 × £15.00

Task 57

Statement	True ✓	False ✓
Employees' pay will increase if more units are produced	✓	
An employee is paid 45p per unit and earns £288 for a production of 640 units (W1)	✓	
An employee who is paid £350 for a production of 875 units is paid 40p per unit (W2)	✓	
Employees paid on a piecework basis will always earn an agreed total amount of pay		✓

Workings:

1   40 × £0.45 = £288
2   350/875 = £0.40 per unit

Task 58

Employee	Hours worked	Units produced	Basic wage £	Bonus £	Gross wage £
L. Singh	42	500	462.00	0	462.00
M. Barton	39	540	429.00	18.00	447.00
S. Valencia	41	508	451.00	4.00	455.00

Workings:

	Basic £	Expected output	Bonus £
L. Singh	42 × £11	42 × 12 = 504 units	(500 – 504) × £0.25 = 0
M. Barton	39 × £11	39 × 12 = 468 units	(540 – 468) × £0.25 = £18.00
S. Valencia	41 × £11	41 × 12 = 492 units	(508 – 492) × £0.25 = £4.00

Task 59

Income/ Expenditure	Budget £	Actual £	Variance £	Adverse or Favourable (A or F)
Income	45,000	40,000	5,000	A
Material	15,800	15,000	800	F
Labour	9,000	8,000	1,000	F
Overheads	8,800	7,500	1,300	F

Assessment objective 4 – Work Effectively in Finance

Task 60

Review the draft letter and identify EIGHT words or collections of letters or digits which are either spelt incorrectly or technically incorrect.

Acount GR45276091

Dear Mrs Gray,

Please find inclosed a current statement for your account. As you will see from the statement, the current account balance for your organisation is £4,725.50. I have been adviced that you have recently placed for goods to the value of £1,750. This order is currently on hold as the extra purchases will result in your credit limit of £5,000 being exceeded.

You are a highly valued customer and I notise that we have not reviewed your credit limit for a number of years. I would therefore suggest that we increase your credit limit to £7,000. If you consider this amount to be insufficient for your current needs please contact me and we can arrange a meeting to review your account.

I would appreciate it if you could make contact as soon as posible so that we can discuss the matter further. I shall be out of the office from next Thursday for a week so if you could contact me before then it would be helpful. I will arrange four the immediate delivery of your outstanding order as soon as I receive your arrangement to the revised credit limit.

I look forward to hearing from you.

Yours faithfully

Task 61

(a) (i)

	Conclusion ✓	Recommendation ✓
For most staff the company briefing explaining the process and timescales for the restructuring of the finance function helped reduce their concerns and the manager kept most staff fully informed of developments and changes during the restructuring.		
Most staff felt that their manager had the time to listen to their concerns during the restructuring process and most staff believe that the new team approach has resulted in increased efficiency of working practices.		
For the wider restructuring, managers need to be trained to ensure that they keep staff fully informed and up to date and that they have the time to listen to their staff's concerns.		✓
Information about job roles and responsibilities, provided to staff prior to the restructuring, was helpful to staff in positioning both their own and colleagues' roles within their team. However, the team building event prior to restructuring was not considered helpful in enabling staff to get to know colleagues within their team.		
Most staff felt that their manager did not keep them fully informed of developments and changes during the restructuring and most staff believe that the new team approach has resulted in increased efficiency of working practices.	✓	

	Conclusion ✓	Recommendation ✓
The team building event held before the finance function restructuring should not be implemented across the organisation as finance staff did not consider it to be helpful in getting to know colleagues within their team.		
For most staff the company briefing explaining the process and timescales for the restructuring of the finance function helped reduce their concerns and the team building event prior to restructuring was considered helpful in enabling staff to get to know colleagues within their team.	✓	
The company briefing explaining the process and timescales for the restructuring of the finance function and the team building event should be features of the wider organisational restructuring as most staff considered they were helpful.		✓
Information about job roles and responsibilities, provided to staff prior to the restructuring, was helpful to staff in identifying both their own and colleagues' roles within their team. However, most felt that their manager did not have the time to listen to their concerns during the restructuring process.	✓	

(ii)

	✓
Results of the questionnaire	
A review of the communications strategy	
A review of the finance function	
A review of restructuring of the finance function	✓
A review of staff perceptions of their manager	

(b)

	✓
Appendices	
Recommendations	
Main body	
Conclusion	
Executive summary	✓
Title	✓

Task 62

(a)

From:	AATstudent@GCCS.com
To:	j.uwaifo@GCCS.com
Subject:	Production expenses October actual compared to budget
Attached:	PDBEOct.xls

Hello John

Paragraph 1

Paragraph 2

Regards

AAT student

	Paragraph 1 ✓	Paragraph 2 ✓
Whilst you spent more on wages at the basic rate of pay you spent less than budget on wages at overtime rate. You spent more than budget on your protective clothing, machine oil and cleaning materials. You spent less than budget on sundry expenses. I hope you find this information useful, if you require any further analysis please do not hesitate to contact me.		
Following the production of the latest month-end report, see attached, I herewith provide you with an analysis of your expenses paid in the month of October. Overall you spent less than budget on your total expenses by £1,645 but this is made up of different expenses in some of which you exceeded budget and in some of which you spent less than budget.		
Whilst you spent less on wages at the basic rate of pay, you spent more than budget on wages at overtime rate. You spent less than budget on your protective clothing and cleaning materials. You spent more than budget on machine oil and sundry expenses. I hope you find this information useful, if you require any further analysis please do not hesitate to contact me.		✓
Following the production of the latest month-end report, see attached, I herewith provide you with an analysis of your expenses paid in the month of October. Overall you spent more than budget on your total expenses by £1,465 but this is made up of different expenses in some of which you exceeded budget and in some of which you spent less than budget.		

	Paragraph 1 ✓	Paragraph 2 ✓
Whilst you spent less on wages at the basic rate of pay you spent less than budget on wages at overtime rate. You spent more than budget on your protective clothing, machine oil and cleaning materials. You spent less than budget on sundry expenses. I hope you find this information useful, if you require any further analysis please do not hesitate to contact me.		
Following the production of the latest month-end report, see attached, I herewith provide you with an analysis of your expenses paid in the month of October. Overall you spent more than budget on your total expenses by £1,645 but this is made up of different expenses in some of which you exceeded budget and in some of which you spent less than budget.	✓	

(b)   It is not necessary to proofread emails if they are sent to people within your organisation but external emails must always be proofread.

> False

The main problem with sending information in an email is that irrespective of the file size only one file may be attached to an email.

> False

Task 63

(a) (i)

Statement	Conclusion ✓	Recommendation ✓
The reduction in actual full-time course fee income when compared to the budget is fully offset by the amount that the actual part-time course fee income exceeds budget.		
The new AAT study programme has been successful in increasing actual part-time course fee income and exceeding the budget, but the actual one-day course fee income is less than the budget.	✓	
The faculty has been successful in reducing the actual cost of books by 25% when compared to the budget, but has overspent on the cost of teaching materials by 5% when compared to the budget.		
The reduction in actual full-time course fee income when compared to the budget is only partially offset by the amount that the actual part-time course fee income exceeds budget.	✓	
The faculty should continue to cover the full-time vacancy with part-time staff as the savings made from the full-time salaries budget are more than twice the additional amount spent in part-time salaries.		✓

Statement	Conclusion ✓	Recommendation ✓
Total actual income is less than the total budgeted income, but total actual expenditure is greater than the total budgeted expenditure.		
The faculty should investigate why the numbers of students registering for part-time courses was less than expected.		
The faculty should increase marketing activity to promote higher numbers of students registering for the one-day practical bookkeeping course and the revision courses.		✓
The reduced numbers of students registering for full-time and one-day courses has led to a reduction in expenditure on registration fees.	✓	

(ii)

	✓
Business and finance budget	
Faculty income and expenditure performance review	
Faculty income and expenditure results	
Review of business and finance faculty income and expenditure against budget	✓
Review of business and finance	

(b)

	✓
Provides suggested actions to overcome the problems identified	
Provides an analysis of the results of the research	✓
Summarises the main points of the research and analysis	
Provides suggested actions to be taken in the future	

(c) When considering the order of a formal business report, which section will usually appear between the executive summary and the main body?

Introduction

Task 64

MEMO

From: AAT student

To: **(1)** David Wright

Date: **(2)** 1 June 20X2

Subject: **(3)** Expense claim deadline

(4) Nigel Allen , accounts department manager, has asked me to inform you that this month, all sales department expense claims relating to **(5)** May 20X2 expenses must be passed to the accounting department by **(6)** 10 June 20X2 at the latest.

This is so that we can ensure all **(7)** sales department employees are reimbursed before the end of **(8)** June 20X2 .

Thanks

AAT student

Task 65

(a)

	✓
Executive Summary	✓
Introduction	
Appendix	
Recommendations Section	

The table is essentially a summary of the key findings so should appear in the executive summary.

(b)

	✓
The majority of the key controls tested are operating effectively.	✓
The majority of the key controls identified are operating effectively.	
The majority of the key controls identified were tested.	✓
Based on the key controls tested, the sales department had the highest percentage of key controls operating effectively.	✓
Based on the key controls identified, the purchasing department had the highest percentage of its key controls tested.	
The same number of key controls were tested in the purchasing department as in the sales department.	

The first conclusion is valid as more than half of the controls **that were tested** were found to be operating effectively in each department. Therefore the majority of those tested are operating effectively.

The second conclusion is not valid. In total only 30 of the 62 key controls **identified** were found to be operating effectively (since the rest were not operating effectively or were not tested). Therefore it is not possible to conclude that the majority of all the key controls are definitely operating effectively (although to say 'based on those tested it is likely they are' is a more reasonable conclusion).

The third conclusion is valid, since 50 of the 62 key controls identified were tested.

The fourth conclusion is also valid. Of the key controls tested in the sales department, 70% (7/10) were found to be operating effectively. This compares to 56% in accounting, 60% in personnel and 58% in purchasing.

The fifth conclusion is not valid, as purchasing only had 86% (12/14) of its identified controls tested. Accounting had 90% (18/20) of its identified controls tested.

The final conclusion is also invalid. 12 key controls were tested in purchasing; only 10 were tested in sales.

(c) There should be an investigation into

> how the ineffective key controls can be modified to ensure they operate effectively.

It is important to the business that the controls are operating effectively (as stated in the task information). Therefore the business should seek to make sure any controls that were found not to be working properly are modified so that they do.

Task 66

(a) Telephone
(b) Email
(c) Face to face discussion
(d) Letter
(e) Email

Task 67

(a)

To:	hgwells@retail.com
From:	acdoyle@southfield.co.uk
Date:	[Today's date]
Subject:	Your recent enquiry
Attach:	Sales brochure.pdf

Hi, Hugh.

Thanks for your msg re our products. Its cool that you were able to come and see our display at the Home Entertainment Trade Fair. More than happy to help with further info.

> Our <u>company's</u> one of the best in the field, and our <u>product's</u> have recently <u>one</u> an award as Retail Product of the Year.
>
> <u>I've</u> attached a brochure <u>what</u> details our full product range. <u>it</u> includes prices and terms of trade. <u>Having</u> received it, I will contact you to see if <u>you'd</u> like to place an order.
>
> In the meantime, <u>me and the sales team</u> are <u>availble</u> to answer any questions you may have. <u>It'd</u> be <u>gr8</u> to hear from you.
>
> <u>Cheers.</u>
>
> <u>Arthur</u>

(b) A more appropriate email would be:

> **To:** hgwells@retail.com
> **From:** acdoyle@southfield.co.uk
> **Date:** [Today's date]
> **Subject:** Your recent enquiry
> **Attach:** Sales brochure.pdf
>
> Dear Mr Wells,
>
> Thank you for your enquiry about our products. I am glad that you were able to come and see our display at the Home Entertainment Trade Fair, and I would be more than happy to help with further information.
>
> Our company is one of the best in the field, and our products have recently won an award as Retail Product of the Year.
>
> I have attached a brochure which details our full product range. It includes prices and terms of trade. Once you have received it, I will contact you to see if you would like to place an order.
>
> In the meantime, the sales team and I are available to answer any questions you may have. We would be glad to hear from you.
>
> Thank you again for your enquiry.
>
> Arthur Doyle
>
> Southfield Electronics
>
> [NB Use the standard signature block for outgoing emails]

Note for explaining changes to Arthur:

Arthur, I've just made a few amendments to your draft email, as you requested. For future reference:

- It is better to use a more formal style with senior individuals and new customers. Don't use first name terms unless they've asked you to. Avoid familiar expressions (like 'cheers'), and keep to a more formal written style (eg 'I have' instead of 'I've').

- In business communications, avoid text message style abbreviations (like 'msg' and 'gr8') and colloquial expressions (like 'cool').

- Remember to check your work for typos (like 'availble') and spelling or grammar related errors (like 'one' instead of 'won').

- You might want to make sure you write in full sentences (which contain a verb and end with a full stop), and look out for errors with clauses and apostrophes.

Task 68

MEMO

To: | Hugh Martin, Accounts Supervisor |

From: Anne Accountant, Accountant

Date: | 20 May 20X1 |

Subject: Bell computers | overcharge | for laptops.

On | 1 May 20X1 | an order (reference | NCA124 |) was placed for five laptop computers which have a list price of | £ | 500 | each. On the same day | Bill Fences |, an account manager at Bell, agreed we would receive a 5% bulk discount because the order was for five or more computers. I enclose my notes from the phone call (including contact details for the account manager) and a copy of the order for your information.

We received invoice (reference | LT241 |) for the computers today which shows the total cost of the laptops to be | £ | 2,500 |. Therefore the anticipated discount of | £ | 125 | has not been applied and we should request that Bell send us a credit note for the original invoice and re-issue a new invoice with the discount applied.

Many thanks for dealing with this.

Anne

Enc: Copies of the order and invoice
Notes of phone call on 1 May 20X1

Task 69

The subject of this report is team working.

A team is a group which works closely together towards a shared goal.

This has a number of benefits:

- Team members each bring their own skills and ideas
- Team members can inspire and motivate each other
- Team working promotes good communication
- The project can benefit from the synergy created by team members

Task 70

To: staff@anycompany.com
From: aatstudent@anycompany.com
Subject: Deadlines

Some issues have arisen recently due to failure to meet deadlines.

Deadlines are set because there is a reason why work needs to be done by a certain time. If you miss your deadline, you may cause somebody else to miss theirs.

If you think that you may not meet a deadline it is important that you let your manager know immediately. Your manager may be able to take action to help you meet your deadline.

Task 71

	✓
Maintaining detailed customer records	
Preparing budgets and forecasts	✓
Sending out supplier statements	

Task 72

	✓
Spreadsheets are used to store and manipulate data.	✓
Spreadsheets can be used for word processing.	
Data in a spreadsheet can be easily updated.	✓
Spreadsheet data can be output in the form of graphs.	✓
Spreadsheets can be used to replace accounting packages.	
Sophisticated databases are making spreadsheets obsolete.	

AAT AQ2016 SAMPLE ASSESSMENT 1 LEVEL 2 SYNOPTIC ASSESSMENT

Time allowed: 2 hours

The AAT may call the assessments on their website,
under study support resources, either a
'practice assessment' or 'sample assessment'.

Level 2 Synoptic Assessment

AAT sample assessment 1

Scenario

The tasks are set in a business situation where the following conditions apply:

- You are employed as an accounts assistant in the finance function at SCM Products.

- The finance function includes the financial and management accounting teams.

- SCM Products uses a manual bookkeeping system.

- Double entry takes place in the general ledger. Individual accounts of trade receivables and trade payables are kept in the sales and purchases ledgers as subsidiary accounts.

- The cash book and petty cash book should be treated as part of the double entry system unless the task instructions state otherwise.

- The VAT rate is 20%.

Task 1 (12 marks)

You work from 9:00am until 2:00pm, Monday to Friday of each week. Each finance period is four weeks in duration so you plan your work in a four week cycle.

The work schedules below show the days when routine tasks must be completed and the amount of time each task takes to complete. It is very important that you complete the management accounts tasks by the end of the identified day and the financial accounts tasks by the day and time indicated.

Monthly work schedule – management accounts				
	Monday	**Tuesday**	**Wednesday**	**Thursday**	**Friday**
Week 1	Material cost report (2 hours)		Material cost report (2 hours)	Budget report (2 hours)	Product cost analysis (1 hour)
Week 2	Labour cost report (2 hours)	Labour cost report (1 hour)	Labour cost report (2 hours)		

Monthly work schedule – management accounts					
	Monday	**Tuesday**	**Wednesday**	**Thursday**	**Friday**
Week 3			Material cost report (1 hour)		Product cost analysis (1 hour)
Week 4	Data gathering (2 hours)			Variance analysis (1 hour)	Cost coding (1 hour)

Weekly work schedule – financial accounts			
Task	**Task to be completed each week by:**		**Task duration**
	Day	**Time**	
Reconcile statements	Friday	13:00	1 hour
Contact customers	Thursday	13:00	2 hours
Process invoices	Friday	11:00	1 hour
Post cheques	Every day	12:00	1 hour
Contact suppliers	Monday	11:00	1 hour
Departmental report	Wednesday	12:00	1 hour
Departmental charges	Tuesday	12:00	2 hours

You are planning your work at the start of the day on Friday of week 4. You have been asked to complete a non-routine cash book task by 10am, which is already included in your to-do list.

(a) Complete your to-do list for today, Friday of week 4. Refer to the management and financial accounts schedules and drag the tasks to be completed into the to-do list below.   (4 marks)

Note. **You may drag each task into the to-do list more than once if the task takes more than one hour to complete.**

Friday, week 4 to-do list	Time
Cash book	09:00–10:00
	10:00–11:00
	11:00–12:00
	12:00–13:00
	13:00–14:00

Tasks:

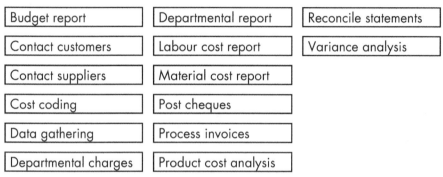

Budget report	Departmental report	Reconcile statements
Contact customers	Labour cost report	Variance analysis
Contact suppliers	Material cost report	
Cost coding	Post cheques	
Data gathering	Process invoices	
Departmental charges	Product cost analysis	

You are often asked to complete non-routine tasks. However, on one day in each four week cycle you are too busy with routine tasks to accept non-routine work.

(b) Identify on which day in which week you will be the busiest with routine tasks from the management and financial accounts schedules. **(2 marks)**

Drag the day of the week and the week number into the table below.

Day of the week	Week number

Days and weeks:

Monday	Wednesday	Friday	Week 1	Week 3
Tuesday	Thursday	Week 2	Week 4	

The non-routine cash book task in today's to-do list is finalising the cash book below for a colleague who has been taken ill.

Cash book

Details	Cash £	Bank £	VAT £	Trade receivables £	Cash sales £	Details	Cash £	Bank £	VAT £	Trade payables £	Cash purchases £
Jaz Shatna	1,110		185		925	Balance b/f		6,542			
Cory Mac		2,150		2,150		P Brady Ltd		1,365		1,365	
P James		1,525		1,525		S Simmons		396	66		330
Cash		850				Cox and Co		234	39		195
						Bank	850				

(c) **What will be the cash and bank balances carried down?**
(4 marks)

Balances	Amount £	Debit ✓	Credit ✓
Cash balance carried down			
Bank balance carried down			

(d) **What will be the totals of the cash and bank columns once the balances have been inserted?** **(2 marks)**

Totals	Amount £
Cash total	
Bank total	

Task 2 (12 marks)

SCM Products has recruited Simon, who has recently left school, to work in the finance function as a trainee. In his first year, Simon will spend time helping you with general tasks such as postal duties, photocopying and filing and he will also work with the cashiers and the management accounting and financial accounting teams.

As Simon is due to start work next week, you have been asked to provide some notes to help him settle into his role. You have decided to begin the notes with the main roles of the finance function.

(a) **From the list below, identify the FOUR main roles of the finance function at SCM Products by dragging them into your notes.** **(4 marks)**

Notes for Simon

Main roles of the finance function:

List of roles:

Ensuring the security of financial data

Ensuring the security of the production processes

Managing funds effectively

Managing staff in other internal departments

Producing monthly bank statements

Producing statutory financial statements

Providing accounting information to other internal departments

Providing IT support to other internal departments

It is Simon's first week and you are helping with his induction into the organisation. You have been asked to highlight important policies and procedures on SCM Products' intranet that Simon should familiarise himself with.

(b) From the list below, identify FOUR policies or procedures Simon should familiarise himself with by dragging them into your notes. **(4 marks)**

Notes for Simon

Policies and procedures you need to be familiar with:

List of policies and procedures:

Holiday entitlement policy

Research and development policy

Product grading procedures

Petty cash claiming procedures

Vehicle maintenance checking procedures

Warehouse storage procedures

Staff development policy

Cheque banking procedures

Simon has been working with you for a few weeks now and you are aware of some concerns in relation to his performance. During meetings, Simon appears uninterested and does not participate. There have also been instances of Simon misunderstanding instructions and not meeting deadlines. You decide to help Simon develop the skills which are important in his role.

(c) **Identify FOUR ways Simon could develop the necessary skills to help him in his role.** **(4 marks)**

Ways for Simon to develop his skills	✓
Interrupt the speaker to ask questions during meetings.	
Make eye contact with the speaker.	
Wait until the person speaking has finished before asking questions.	
Cough loudly to indicate to the speaker that the meeting has overrun.	
Complete work tasks at your own pace, focussing on the accuracy of the work.	
Discuss difficulties in meeting deadlines with your supervisor at the earliest opportunity.	
Complete work tasks as quickly as possible, relying on your supervisor to check the accuracy of the work.	
Ask as many questions as you need until you fully understand what you are being asked to do.	

Task 3 (12 marks)

SCM Products has supplied goods to Peppers Ltd. You have been asked to complete the invoice by calculating the invoice amounts.

(a) **Refer to the price list and complete the FOUR boxes in the invoice below.** **(4 marks)**

Invoice

SCM Products
14 London Road
Parton. PA21 7NL
VAT Registration No. 298 3827 04

Invoice No. 3912

To: Peppers Ltd
121 New Street
Grangeton, GX12 4SD

Invoice date: 15 May 20XX
Delivery date: 13 May 20XX
Customer account code: PEP003

Quantity of units	Product code	Price each £	Net amount £	VAT amount £	Total amount £
120	BXC20				

Terms of payment: Net monthly account

Price list

Product code	Price each £
ACG10	5.53
BCF15	2.75
BXC20	3.85
CXC20	1.52
DFJ15	3.75
DFJ20	4.98

Your next task is to enter the invoice into the appropriate daybook.

(b) **Record the invoice in the correct daybook by:** **(6 marks)**

- **Selecting the correct daybook title; and**
- **Making the necessary entries.**

▼

Drop-down list:

Cash book
Discounts received daybook
Petty cash book
Purchases daybook
Purchases returns daybook
Sales daybook
Sales returns daybook

Date 20XX	Details	Account code	Invoice number	Total £	VAT £	Net £
15 May	▼		3912			

Picklist:

Peppers Ltd
SCM Products

SCM Products is considering offering its customers a 2.5% prompt payment discount for payment within five days of date of invoice.

(c) **Calculate the amount that would be paid by Peppers Ltd if a 2.5% prompt payment discount was offered on the invoice in (a) and the invoice paid within five days.** **(1 mark)**

£

(d) **What is the latest date by which SCM Products should receive the payment from Peppers Ltd if the prompt payment discount was taken?** **(1 mark)**

▼

Drop-down list:

13 May 20XX
15 May 20XX
18 May 20XX
20 May 20XX
30 May 20XX

Task 4 (16 marks)

You are working on the sales and purchase ledger control accounts at the end of June.

The debit entries in the sales ledger control account total £219,476 and the credit entries total £197,823.

(a) **Calculate the amount of the balance brought down on 1 July.**

£	

You now need to reconcile the sales ledger control account with the sales ledger.

You have already totalled the balances of each account in the sales ledger and recorded a total of £19,812, but you have just discovered that you omitted the balances of the sales ledger accounts below.

Cooper Ltd

Details	Amount £	Details	Amount £
Balance b/f	1,746		

Sophie Hunt

Details	Amount £	Details	Amount £
		Balance b/f	312

(b) **Calculate the total of the sales ledger balances including the two accounts above.**

£	

(c) **What is the difference between the balance of the sales ledger control account you calculated in (a) and the total of the sales ledger balances you calculated in (b)?**

£	

(d) **Identify which ONE of the reasons below could explain the difference you calculated in (c).**

Reason	✓
Irrecoverable debts written off were recorded twice in the sales ledger control account.	
Goods sold were recorded twice in the sales ledger.	
Goods returned were recorded twice in the sales ledger control account.	
Discounts allowed were recorded twice in the sales ledger.	

Your next task is to prepare the purchase ledger control account.

You have been given the totals of the purchases, purchase returns and discounts received daybooks.

Purchase daybook extract

Date 20XX	Details	Total £	VAT £	Net £
30 Jun	Totals	23,454	3,909	19,545

Purchase returns daybook extract

Date 20XX	Details	Total £	VAT £	Net £
30 Jun	Totals	2,898	483	2,415

Discounts received daybook extract

Date 20XX	Details	Total £	VAT £	Net £
30 Jun	Totals	768	128	640

(e) **What will be the entries in the purchase ledger control account?**

Balances	Amount £	Debit ✓	Credit ✓
Entry from the purchases daybook			
Entry from the purchases returns daybook			
Entry from the discounts received daybook			

You now need to deal with the note below which you have received today, 30 June 20XX, from the Finance Manager, Paul Page.

Note

> I am concerned that the balance of £1,746 owing from Cooper Ltd, a credit customer, is overdue for payment.
>
> The amount outstanding relates to invoice number 328 dated 12 March 20XX.
>
> Please prepare a letter for Mr Cooper at Cooper Ltd, ready for my signature, explaining the situation and asking him to contact me if there are any issues, or to send payment by return.
>
> Thanks
>
> Paul

(f) **Prepare an appropriate business letter to Cooper Ltd, making sure you include all relevant information.**

SCM Products
14 London Road, Parton, PA21 7NL
Telephone: 01956 492104
Email: info@scmproducts.co.uk

Mr Cooper
Cooper Ltd
12 The Hollow
Lakton, LK8 4DS

Task 5 (12 marks)

SCM Products is committed to improving its Corporate Social Responsibility (CSR) activities. You are part of a team that has been asked to assist in the preparation of an annual report detailing the CSR initiatives planned.

(a) **Drag THREE appropriate initiatives into EACH section of the Corporate Social Responsibility report below.** **(6 marks)**

SCM Products
Corporate Social Responsibility Report

Our commitment to minimising the environmental impact of our activities.

Initiatives planned:

Our commitment to improving the welfare of our employees.

Initiatives planned:

Initiatives:

Ensuring staff use public transport rather than their own vehicles when travelling for business purposes.

Ensuring production processes maximise energy consumption.

Ensuring all staff minimise costs and expenses to the organisation.

Introducing flexible working conditions so staff can work and still meet personal commitments.

Ensuring all staff complete overtime each month.

Imposing a weekend working requirement on all staff.

Increasing senior management salaries by 10%.

Offering free membership to a local gymnasium for all staff.

Ensuring emissions from our delivery vehicles are minimised.

Allowing staff to complete overseas projects which bring water to communities in developing countries.

Installing energy saving equipment in our production plant.

Offering staff training and supporting those wishing to gain further qualifications.

In line with a previous commitment to improving the local environment, SCM Products recently held an event to raise funds to renovate a local community centre. The CSR team is responsible for reporting on the costs of the event.

The budgeted costs were:

Food: £1.75 per person
Entertainment: £50 per hundred people

1,500 people attended the event. The actual costs are shown in the table below and you have been asked to compare these with the budgeted costs.

(b) Complete the table below by: (6 marks)
- **Inserting the total budgeted amount for each cost**
- **Inserting the variance for each cost**
- **Selecting whether each variance is adverse or favourable**

Event cost performance report				
Cost	Budget £	Actual £	Variance £	Adverse/Favourable
Food		2,200		[▼]
Entertainment		1,150		[▼]

Drop-down list:

Adverse
Favourable

Task 6 (24 marks)

Your manager at SCM Products is interested in how costs behave at different levels of output. She has asked you to prepare a cost analysis at different levels of output for a product. You are told that fixed costs are £20,000 and variable costs are £5 per unit.

(a) Complete the table below to show fixed, variable and total and unit costs for each of the three levels of output. (12 marks)

Level of output	Fixed costs £	Variable costs £	Total costs £	Unit cost £
2,000 units				
5,000 units				
8,000 units				

(b) In the box below, write a short report for non-finance staff containing:

- A brief introduction outlining the areas you will be covering in the report

- An explanation of what a fixed cost is, giving an example

- An explanation of what a variable cost is, giving an example

- A description of what happens to the unit cost as output increases and the reason for this

Your report must be clear and structured appropriately.

(12 marks)

Task 7 (12 marks)

You are preparing for the accounting month end at SCM Products.

Your first task is to transfer data from the purchases daybook to the ledgers. An extract from the purchases daybook is shown below.

Purchases daybook

Date 20XX	Details	Invoice number	Total £	VAT £	Net £
31 Aug	Carstairs Ltd	C1673X	474	79	395

(a) Show whether the entries in the general ledger will be debit or credit entries. **(3 marks)**

Account name	Debit ✓	Credit ✓
Purchases		
VAT		
Purchases ledger control		

(b) What will be the entry in the purchases ledger? **(3 marks)**

Account name	Amount £	Debit ✓	Credit ✓
▼			

Drop-down list:

Carstairs Ltd
Purchases
Purchases ledger control
Purchases returns
Sales
Sales ledger control
Sales returns
VAT

You have found an error in the accounting records. A cheque payment of £4,206 to a credit supplier has been recorded as £4,260.

You have partially prepared journal entries to correct the error in the general ledger.

(c) **Complete the journals below by:** **(4 marks)**
- **Removing the incorrect entries; and**
- **Recording the correct entries.**

Do not enter a zero in unused debit or credit column cells.

Journal to remove the incorrect entries

Account name	Debit £	Credit £
Bank		
Purchases ledger control		

Journal to record the correct entries

Account name	Debit £	Credit £
Purchases ledger control		
Bank		

You have also identified that discounts received were omitted from the general ledger. You have prepared the journal entries below to correct the omission

Journal

Account name	Debit £	Credit £
Purchases ledger control	120	
Discounts received		120

(d) **Record the journal in the general ledger by dragging the appropriate entry into each account below.** **(2 marks)**

Discounts received

Details	Amount £	Details	Amount £
		Balance b/f	993

Purchases ledger control

Details	Amount £	Details	Amount £
		Balance b/f	37,721

Entries:

Discount received	120

Purchases ledger control	120

AAT AQ2016 SAMPLE ASSESSMENT 1 LEVEL 2 SYNOPTIC ASSESSMENT

ANSWERS

Level 2 Synoptic Assessment

AAT sample assessment 1

Task 1 (12 marks)

You work from 09.00 until 14.00, Monday to Friday of each week. Each finance period is four weeks in duration so you plan your work in a four week cycle.

The work schedules below show the days when routine tasks must be completed and the amount of time each task takes to complete. It is very important that you complete the management accounts tasks by the end of the identified day and the financial accounts tasks by the day and time indicated.

Monthly work schedule – management accounts				
	Monday	**Tuesday**	**Wednesday**	**Thursday**	**Friday**
Week 1	Material cost report (2 hours)		Material cost report (2 hours)	Budget report (2 hours)	Product cost analysis (1 hour)
Week 2	Labour cost report (2 hours)	Labour cost report (1 hour)	Labour cost report (2 hours)		
Week 3			Material cost report (1 hour)		Product cost analysis (1 hour)
Week 4	Data gathering (2 hours)			Variance analysis (1 hour)	Cost coding (1 hour)

Weekly work schedule – financial accounts			
Task	**Task to be completed each week by:**		**Task duration**
	Day	**Time**	
Reconcile statements	Friday	13:00	1 hour
Contact customers	Thursday	13:00	2 hours
Process invoices	Friday	11:00	1 hour
Post cheques	Every day	12:00	1 hour
Contact suppliers	Monday	11:00	1 hour
Departmental report	Wednesday	12:00	1 hour
Departmental charges	Tuesday	12:00	2 hours

You are planning your work at the start of the day on Friday of week 4. You have been asked to complete a non-routine cash book task by 10am, which is already included in your to-do list.

(a) **Complete your to-do list for today, Friday of week 4. Refer to the management and financial accounts schedules and drag the tasks to be completed into the to-do list below.** **(4 marks)**

Note. **You may drag each task into the to-do list more than once if the task takes more than one hour to complete.**

Friday, week 4 to-do list	Time
Cash book	09:00–10:00
Process invoices	10:00–11:00
Post cheques	11:00–12:00
Reconcile statements	12:00–13:00
Cost coding	13:00–14:00

Tasks:

Budget report	Departmental report	Reconcile statements
Contact customers	Labour cost report	Variance analysis
Contact suppliers	Material cost report	
Cost coding	Post cheques	
Data gathering	Process invoices	
Departmental charges	Product cost analysis	

You are often asked to complete non-routine tasks. However, on one day in each four week cycle you are too busy with routine tasks to accept non-routine work.

(b) **Identify on which day in which week you will be the busiest with routine tasks from the management and financial accounts schedules.** **(2 marks)**

Drag the day of the week and the week number into the table below.

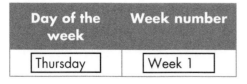

Day of the week	Week number
Thursday	Week 1

Days and weeks:

Monday	Wednesday	Friday	Week 1	Week 3

Tuesday	Thursday	Week 2	Week 4

The non-routine cash book task in today's to-do list is finalising the cash book below for a colleague who has been taken ill.

Cash book

Details	Cash £	Bank £	VAT £	Trade receivables £	Cash sales £	Details	Cash £	Bank £	VAT £	Trade payables £	Cash purchases £
Jaz Shatna	1,110		185		925	Balance b/f		6,542			
Cory Mac		2,150		2,150		P Brady Ltd		1,365		1,365	
P James		1,525		1,525		S Simmons		396	66		330
Cash		850				Cox and Co		234	39		195
						Bank	850				

(c) What will be the cash and bank balances carried down?
(4 marks)

Balances	Amount £	Debit ✓	Credit ✓
Cash balance carried down	260		✓
Bank balance carried down	4,012	✓	

(d) What will be the totals of the cash and bank columns once the balances have been inserted? **(2 marks)**

Totals	Amount £
Cash total	1,110
Bank total	8,537

Task 2 (12 marks)

SCM Products has recruited Simon, who has recently left school, to work in the finance function as a trainee. In his first year, Simon will spend time helping you with general tasks such as postal duties, photocopying and filing and he will also work with the cashiers and the management accounting and financial accounting teams.

As Simon is due to start work next week, you have been asked to provide some notes to help him settle into his role. You have decided to begin the notes with the main roles of the finance function.

(a) **From the list below, identify the FOUR main roles of the finance function at SCM Products by dragging them into your notes.** **(4 marks)**

> **Notes for Simon**
>
> **Main roles of the finance function:**
>
> | Ensuring the security of financial data |
> | --- |
> | Managing funds effectively |
> | Producing statutory financial statements |
> | Providing accounting information to other internal departments |

List of roles:

Ensuring the security of the production processes

Managing staff in other internal departments

Producing monthly bank statements

Providing IT support to other internal departments

It is Simon's first week and you are helping with his induction into the organisation. You have been asked to highlight important policies and procedures on SCM Products' intranet that Simon should familiarise himself with.

(b) **From the list below, identify FOUR policies or procedures Simon should familiarise himself with by dragging them into your notes.** **(4 marks)**

Notes for Simon

Policies and procedures you need to be familiar with:

Holiday entitlement policy

Petty cash claiming procedures

Staff development policy

Cheque banking procedures

List of policies and procedures:

Research and development policy

Product grading procedures

Vehicle maintenance checking procedures

Warehouse storage procedures

Simon has been working with you for a few weeks now and you are aware of some concerns in relation to his performance. During meetings, Simon appears uninterested and does not participate. There have also been instances of Simon misunderstanding instructions and not meeting deadlines. You decide to help Simon develop the skills which are important in his role.

(c) **Identify FOUR ways Simon could develop the necessary skills to help him in his role.** **(4 marks)**

Ways for Simon to develop his skills	✓
Interrupt the speaker to ask questions during meetings.	
Make eye contact with the speaker.	✓
Wait until the person speaking has finished before asking questions.	✓
Cough loudly to indicate to the speaker that the meeting has overrun.	
Complete work tasks at your own pace, focussing on the accuracy of the work.	
Discuss difficulties in meeting deadlines with your supervisor at the earliest opportunity.	✓
Complete work tasks as quickly as possible, relying on your supervisor to check the accuracy of the work.	
Ask as many questions as you need until you fully understand what you are being asked to do.	✓

Task 3 (12 marks)

SCM Products has supplied goods to Peppers Ltd. You have been asked to complete the invoice by calculating the invoice amounts.

(a) **Refer to the price list and complete the FOUR boxes in the invoice below.** **(4 marks)**

Invoice

SCM Products
14 London Road
Parton. PA21 7NL
VAT Registration No. 298 3827 04

Invoice No. 3912

To: Peppers Ltd
121 New Street
Grangeton, GX12 4SD

Invoice date: 15 May 20XX
Delivery date: 13 May 20XX
Customer account code: PEP003

Quantity of units	Product code	Price each £	Net amount £	VAT amount £	Total amount £
120	BXC20	3.85	462	92.40	554.40

Terms of payment: Net monthly account

Price list

Product code	Price each £
ACG10	5.53
BCF15	2.75
BXC20	3.85
CXC20	1.52
DFJ15	3.75
DFJ20	4.98

Your next task is to enter the invoice into the appropriate daybook.

(b) **Record the invoice in the correct daybook by:** **(6 marks)**

 – **Selecting the correct daybook title; and**
 – **Making the necessary entries.**

Sales daybook

Date 20XX	Details	Account code	Invoice number	Total £	VAT £	Net £
15 May	Peppers Ltd	PEP003	3912	554.40	92.40	462

SCM Products is considering offering its customers a 2.5% prompt payment discount for payment within five days of date of invoice.

(c) **Calculate the amount that would be paid by Peppers Ltd if a 2.5% prompt payment discount was offered on the invoice in (a) and the invoice paid within five days.** **(1 mark)**

£ | 540.54

(d) **What is the latest date by which SCM Products should receive the payment from Peppers Ltd if the prompt payment discount was taken?** **(1 mark)**

20 May 20XX

....

Task 4 (16 marks)

(a) **Calculate the amount of the balance brought down 1 July.**
(1 mark)

£ | 21,653

(b) **Calculate the total of the sales ledger balances including the two accounts above.** **(1 mark)**

£ | 21,246

(c) **What is the difference between the balance of the sales ledger control account you calculated in (a) and the total of the sales ledger balances you calculated in (b)?** **(1 mark)**

£ | 407

(d) **Identify which ONE of the reasons below could explain the difference you calculated in (c).** **(1 mark)**

Reason	✓
Irrecoverable debts written off were recorded twice in the sales ledger control account.	
Goods sold were recorded twice in the sales ledger.	
Goods returned were recorded twice in the sales ledger control account.	
Discounts allowed were recorded twice in the sales ledger.	✓

(e) **What will be the entries in the purchase ledger control account?** **(6 marks)**

Balances	Amount £	Debit ✓	Credit ✓
Entry from the purchases daybook	23,454		✓
Entry from the purchases returns daybook	2,898	✓	
Entry from the discounts received daybook	768	✓	

(f) **Prepare an appropriate business letter to Cooper Ltd, making sure you include all relevant information.** **(6 marks)**

SCM Products
14 London Road, Parton, PA21 7NL
Telephone: 01956 492104
email: info@scmproducts.co.uk

Mr Cooper
Cooper Ltd
12 The Hollow
Lakton, LK8 4DS
30 June 20XX

Dear Mr Cooper,

Overdue Account

It has come to my attention that your account is overdue for payment.

The outstanding amount of £1,746 relates to invoice number 328 dated 12 March 20XX.

If you have any queries regarding this invoice please contact me to discuss the matter.

Otherwise I look forward to receiving your payment by return.

Your sincerely,

Paul Page
Finance Manager

Marks	Descriptor
0	No response worthy of credit

1–2	• There is some form of opening salutation and complimentary close, although they are not necessarily consistent with each other.
	
	• The body of the letter is sufficiently grammatically correct to communicate the message that:
	
	  – An amount is overdue/outstanding
	  – Payment is required by return
	
	• The letter, including the opening salutation and complimentary close, may contain spelling errors.

3–4	• The letter is dated, including the year, and has an appropriate heading.
	
	• The opening salutation and complimentary close are appropriate and consistent with each other.
	
	• Paul Page's name is shown below the complimentary close.
	
	• The spelling and grammar within the body of the letter is sufficiently correct to communicate the message that:
	
	  – An amount of £1,746 is overdue/outstanding
	
	  – The customer should contact Paul Page to discuss any queries or forward payment by return

5–6	• The letter is dated, including the year, and has an appropriate heading.
	• The opening salutation and complimentary close are appropriate and consistent with each other.
	• Paul Page's name and job title are shown below the complimentary close.
	• The body of the letter is well structured, with spelling and grammar that is mainly correct and communicates the message that:
	– An amount of £1,746 is overdue/outstanding
	– The amount overdue/outstanding relates to invoice number 328 dated 12 March 20XX
	– The customer should contact Paul Page to discuss any queries or forward payment by return

Task 5 (12 marks)

SCM Products is committed to improving its Corporate Social Responsibility (CSR) activities. You are part of a team that has been asked to assist in the preparation of an annual report detailing the CSR initiatives planned.

(a) **Drag THREE appropriate initiatives into EACH section of the Corporate Social Responsibility report below.** **(6 marks)**

SCM Products
Corporate Social Responsibility Report
Our commitment to minimising the environmental impact of our activities. Initiatives planned:
Ensuring staff use public transport rather than their own vehicles when travelling for business purposes.
Ensuring emission from our delivery vehicles are minimised.
Installing energy saving equipment in our production plant.

Our commitment to improving the welfare of our employees.

Initiatives planned:

Introducing flexible working conditions so staff can work and still meet personal commitments.

Offering free membership to a local gymnasium for all staff.

Offering staff training and supporting those wishing to gain further qualifications.

Initiatives:

Ensuring production processes maximise energy consumption.

Ensuring all staff minimise costs and expenses to the organisation.

Ensuring all staff complete overtime each month.

Imposing a weekend working requirement on all staff.

Increasing senior management salaries by 10%.

Allowing staff to complete overseas projects which bring water to communities in developing countries.

In line with a previous commitment to improving the local environment, SCM Products recently held an event to raise funds to renovate a local community centre. The CSR team is responsible for reporting on the costs of the event.

The budgeted costs were:

Food: £1.75 per person
Entertainment: £50 per hundred people

1,500 people attended the event. The actual costs are shown in the table below and you have been asked to compare these with the budgeted costs.

(b) **Complete the table below by:** **(6 marks)**

- **Inserting the total budgeted amount for each cost**
- **Inserting the variance for each cost**
- **Selecting whether each variance is adverse or favourable**

Event cost performance report				
Cost	Budget £	Actual £	Variance £	Adverse/Favourable
Food	2,625	2,200	425	Favourable
Entertainment	750	1,150	400	Adverse

Task 6 (24 marks)

Your manager at SCM Products is interested in how costs behave at different levels of output. She has asked you to prepare a cost analysis at different levels of output for a product. You are told that fixed costs are £20,000 and variable costs are £5 per unit.

(a) **Complete the table below to show fixed, variable and total and unit costs for each of the three levels of output. (12 marks)**

Level of output	Fixed costs £	Variable costs £	Total costs £	Unit cost £
2,000 units	20,000	10,000	30,000	15.00
5,000 units	20,000	25,000	45,000	9.00
8,000 units	20,000	40,000	60,000	7.50

(b) **In the box below, write a short report for non-finance staff containing:**

- **A brief introduction outlining the areas you will be covering in the report**

- **An explanation of what a fixed cost is, giving an example**

- **An explanation of what a variable cost is, giving an example**

- **A description of what happens to the unit cost as output increases and the reason for this**

Your report must be clear and structured appropriately.
(12 marks)

> ### Introduction
>
> This report:
>
> - Explains and gives examples of fixed and variable costs
> - Describes the effect of increased output on unit cost
>
> ### Fixed cost
>
> A fixed cost is one that remains the same irrespective of the level of output. An example of a fixed cost for a factory would be the cost of rent.
>
> ### Variable cost
>
> A variable cost is one which changes in relation to the level of output. An example of a variable production cost would be the direct materials used in a product.
>
> ### Description of what happens to the cost per unit as output increases
>
> The cost per unit decreases as output increases. This is because fixed costs do not change with output so are shared between an increased number of units when output increases.

Introduction up to 2 marks. Content must include all of the **three** areas to be covered in the report (1 mark) plus a further mark for a coherent introduction, which is correctly spelt and is grammatically correct.

Fixed costs up to 2 marks. One mark for explanation of fixed cost and for a clear example (must not be ambiguous). Up to a further mark for suitable sentence construction and clarity of writing without spelling mistakes and using correct grammar.

Variable costs up to 2 marks. One mark for explanation of variable cost and for a clear example (must not be ambiguous). Up to a further mark for suitable sentence construction and clarity of writing without spelling mistakes and using correct grammar.

Cost per unit up to 4 marks. One mark for stating what happens to the cost per unit. One mark for a clear description of why this happens. Up to a further **two** marks for suitable sentence construction and clarity of writing without spelling mistakes and using correct grammar.

Task 7 (12 marks)

You are preparing for the accounting month end at SCM Products.

Your first task is to transfer data from the purchases daybook to the ledgers. An extract from the purchases daybook is shown below.

Purchases daybook

Date 20XX	Details	Invoice number	Total £	VAT £	Net £
31 Aug	Carstairs Ltd	C1673X	474	79	395

(a) **Show whether the entries in the general ledger will be debit or credit entries.** **(3 marks)**

Account name	Debit ✓	Credit ✓
Purchases	✓	
VAT	✓	
Purchases ledger control		✓

(b) **What will be the entry in the purchases ledger?** **(3 marks)**

Account name	Amount £	Debit ✓	Credit ✓
Carstairs Ltd	474		✓

You have found an error in the accounting records. A cheque payment of £4,206 to a credit supplier has been recorded as £4,260.

You have partially prepared journal entries to correct the error in the general ledger.

(c) **Complete the journals below by:** **(4 marks)**

- **Removing the incorrect entries; and**
- **Recording the correct entries.**

Do not enter a zero in unused debit or credit column cells.

Journal to remove the incorrect entries

Account name	Debit £	Credit £
Bank	4,260	
Purchases ledger control		4,260

Journal to record the correct entries

Account name	Debit £	Credit £
Purchases ledger control	4,206	
Bank		4,206

You have also identified that discounts received were omitted from the general ledger. You have prepared the journal entries below to correct the omission.

Journal

Account name	Debit £	Credit £
Purchases ledger control	120	
Discounts received		120

(d) **Record the journal in the general ledger by dragging the appropriate entry into each account below.** **(2 marks)**

Discounts received

Details	Amount £	Details	Amount £
		Balance b/f	993
		Purchases ledger control	120

Purchases ledger control

Details	Amount £	Details	Amount £
Discount received	120	Balance b/f	37,721

Entries:

Discount received	120

Purchases ledger control	120

AAT AQ2016 SAMPLE ASSESSMENT 2
LEVEL 2 SYNOPTIC ASSESSMENT

You are advised to attempt sample assessment 2 online from the AAT website. This will ensure you are prepared for how the assessment will be presented on the AAT's system when you attempt the real assessment. Please access the assessment using the address below:

https://www.aat.org.uk/training/study-support/search

The AAT may call the assessments on their website, under study support resources, either a 'practice assessment' or 'sample assessment'.

BPP PRACTICE ASSESSMENT 1
LEVEL 2 SYNOPTIC
ASSESSMENT

Time allowed: 2 hours

Level 2 Synoptic Assessment
BPP practice assessment 1

Task 1

It is important to understand you will be required to follow policies and procedures in the completion of your work and why it is important to adhere to organisational policies and procedures.

(a)   Which ONE of the following policies and procedures is most likely to be relevant to those working in an accounting function?

	✓
Production quality control policy	
Website development procedures	
Staff code of behaviour policy	
Motor vehicle maintenance policy	

(b)   Identify which TWO of the following statements are correct:

	✓
Organisations, by law, must have at least ten policies and procedures.	
It is good practice for organisations to have policies and procedures so all staff work to a consistent standard.	
Data protection policy is an example of a policy that would not apply to those staff working in an accounting function.	
Organisational procedures always result in staff taking longer to do work tasks.	
Ensuring staff adhere to organisational policies and procedures should result in more efficient working practices.	
The Health and Safety policy only applies to those working in the production department.	

Those working in an accounting function will have to communicate with both internal and external stakeholders.

(c) **Identify which TWO of the following stakeholders a trainee in the accounting function is most likely to communicate with on a regular basis.**

Complete the answer by writing the correct stakeholders in the box provided.

Stakeholders an accounting trainee is most likely to communicate with on a regular basis

Stakeholders:

Chairperson of the local AAT branch

Government ministers

Trade receivables

Trade union representative

HM Revenue & Customs

People living close to the organisation's offices

The following are the requirements for the accounting function meeting:

Date: 18 August 20XX	Time: 10:00am–2.00pm	Tea/coffee required: NO Time: N/A	Lunch IS required Time: 12:00
Purpose: The monthly accounting function review meeting.			
Number of attendees: 25 plus Finance Director and Managing Director.			
Special requirements: Two members of staff require vegetarian food, no other special dietary requirements.			
Room configuration: Usual, horseshoe style please.			
Other information: We require an overhead projector, white screen and laptop.			
Cost to be charged to: Mr John Brean		Budget Code: ACC3217653	

Your manager (John Brean) has asked you to email the Facilities Manager to advise him of the requirements for the monthly accounting function review meeting.

(d) **Complete the email below to book the meeting with the Facilities Manager Martin Slone (mslone@Mbs.com) by inserting the email address of the recipient and selecting TWO paragraphs that should be inserted into the main body of the email to make all the arrangements for the meeting.**

From: AATstudent@Mbs.com

To:

Subject: Meeting room booking

Hello Martin

Paragraph 1

Paragraph 2

Regards

AAT student

	Paragraph 1 ✓	Paragraph 2 ✓
We require a room for our review meeting on 18 August 20XX between 10:00am and 2:00pm. Tea/coffee is not required but lunch is required at 12:00pm. Two people require vegetarian food; the others have no special dietary requirements.		
The room should be arranged in a horseshoe style and an overhead projector, wide screen and laptop will be required for the meeting. The costs associated with the meeting are to be sent for the attention of John Brean. Budget code AC3217653 should be charged.		
The accounting function needs a room for its monthly review meeting on 18 August 20XX. The meeting is due to start at 10:00am and should finish at 2:00pm. There will be 25 people at the meeting and we shall require lunch at 12:00pm; two attendees require vegetarian food, nobody else has any special dietary arrangements. There will not be a requirement for tea or coffee.		

	Paragraph 1 ✓	Paragraph 2 ✓
On behalf of John Brean I write to request a booking for the accounting's function monthly review meeting. There will be 25 staff including the Finance Director and Managing Director attending the meeting and lunch will be required at 12:00pm. The only special dietary requirements are that two people require vegetarian food. Tea/coffee will not be required.		
An overhead projector, white screen and laptop will be required for the meeting. The room should be arranged in our usual style. The costs associated with the meeting are to be sent for the attention of John Brean. Budget code AC3217653 should be charged.		
An overhead projector, white screen and laptop will be required for the meeting. The costs associated with the meeting are to be sent for the attention of John Brean. Budget code ACC3217653 should be charged.		
We will require an overhead projector, white screen and laptop for the meeting. The room should be arranged in our usual horseshoe style. The costs associated with the meeting are to be sent for the attention of John Brean. Budget code ACC3217653 should be charged.		
Please arrange for a room to be booked for the accounting function's monthly review meeting. There will be 25 staff plus the Finance Director and Managing Director at the meeting between 10:00am and 2:00pm on 18 August 20XX. Tea/coffee will not be required and lunch is requested at 12:00pm. Two people require vegetarian food; there are no dietary requirements.		

(e) Identify whether the following statements are true or false:

You do not need to proofread emails as this is an informal method of communication.

	▼

Picklist:

True
False

When deciding upon the best method of communication you only need to consider the information you are trying to communicate.

	▼

Picklist:

True
False

Task 2

Costing uses a number of techniques to assist management.

(a) Identify the following statements as being true or false by putting a tick in the relevant column of the table below.

Statement	True ✓	False ✓
FIFO is a technique used to cost issues and to value inventories		
The piecework method to pay labour guarantees a set amount of wages		
A variance calculation measures the difference between revenue and cost		
Classification of cost by behaviour allows the planning of total cost at differing levels of output		

The following table lists some of the characteristics of financial accounting and management accounting.

(b) **Indicate the characteristics for each system by putting a tick in the relevant column of the table below.**

Characteristic	Financial accounting ✓	Management accounting ✓
This system produces statements that are used as a basis to determine the tax charge		
This system uses techniques to cost issues and to value inventories		
This system produces statements that are primarily for internal use		
This system produces statements that have many external users		

Task 3

The following credit transactions have been entered into the sales returns day book as shown below. No entries have yet been made into the ledgers.

Sales returns day-book

Date 20XX	Details	Credit note number	Total £	VAT £	Net £
30 Jun	Wem Designs	CN221	1,128	188	940
30 Jun	Bailey and Byng	CN222	354	59	295
	Totals		1,482	247	1,235

(a) **What will be the entries in the sales ledger?**

Sales ledger

Account name	Amount £	Debit	Credit
▼			
▼			

Picklist:

Bailey and Byng
Purchases
Purchases ledger control
Purchases returns
Sales
Sales ledger control
Sales returns
VAT
Wem Designs

(b) **What will be the entries in the general ledger?**

General ledger

Account name	Amount £	Debit	Credit
▼			
▼			
▼			

Picklist:

Bailey and Byng
Purchases
Purchases ledger control
Purchases returns
Sales
Sales ledger control
Sales returns
VAT
Wem Designs

(c) The following is the account of J B Mills in the sales ledger at 30 June 20XX.

(i) Insert the balance carried down together with date and details.

(ii) Insert the totals.

(iii) Insert the balance brought down together with date and details.

J B Mills

Date 20XX	Details	Amount £	Date 20XX	Details	Amount £
1 Jun	Balance b/d	1,585	22 Jun	Bank	678
11 Jun	Invoice 1269	1,804	29 Jun	Credit note 049	607
▼		▼	▼		▼
	Total			Total	
▼		▼	▼		▼

Picklist:

30 Jun
1 July
Balance b/d
Balance c/d

Task 4

You are employed in an accountancy practice called ABC, and have been given responsibility for a new client that is to trade as Khan Catering.

As Khan Catering is a new business a new set of accounts is to be opened. A partially completed journal to record the opening entries is shown below.

(a) Complete the journal by showing whether each amount would be in the debit or credit column.

Account name	Amount £	Debit ✓	Credit ✓
Capital	4,780		
Office expenses	1,927		
Sales	8,925		
Purchases	4,212		
Commission received	75		
Discounts received	54		
Cash at bank	1,814		
Petty cash	180		
Loan from bank	5,000		
Motor expenses	372		
Motor vehicles	9,443		
Other expenses	886		
Journal to record opening entries of new business.			

You are now required to respond to the email below which you have just received from your supervisor Jack Sterling.

From:	Jacksterling@ABC.com
To:	Accountingtechnician@ABC.com
Cc:	
Subject:	Purpose of the journal and its entries
Date:	01/08/20XX

Hello (your name)

Thank you for completing the journal entry task this morning.

Jessica Khan, the owner of the business, has sent me an email asking for an explanation of the purpose of a journal, and the types of entries that can be recorded.

I am in meetings this afternoon, so could you please respond to Jessica on my behalf? Jessica has mentioned that she would like to receive a response by the end of today.

I would be grateful if you would copy me in to your reply.

Jessica's email address is: Khancatering@info.com

Many thanks,

Regards,

Jack

Jack Sterling

Office Supervisor

(b) **In accordance with your supervisor's instructions, prepare an email to be sent to Jessica Khan.**

From: Accountingtechnician@ABC.com

To:

Cc:

Subject:

Date:

Task 5

Gold pays its employees by BACS transfer every month and maintains a wages control account. A summary of last month's payroll transactions is shown below:

Payroll transactions	£
Gross wages	21,999
Income tax	5,755
Employer's NI	1,649
Employees' NI	1,476
Employees' pension contributions	750

(a) **Show the journal entries needed in the general ledger to record the wages expense.**

Account name	Amount £	Debit ✓	Credit ✓
▼			
▼			

Picklist:

Bank
Employees' NI
Employer's NI
HM Revenue and Customs
Income tax
Net wages
Pension
Wages control
Wages expense

(b) **Show the journal entries needed in the general ledger to record the net wages paid to employees.**

Account name	Amount £	Debit ✓	Credit ✓
▼			
▼			

Picklist:

Bank
Employees' NI
Employer's NI
HM Revenue and Customs
Income tax
Net wages
Pension
Wages control
Wages expense

Task 6

You are a trainee in the accounting function and you work for both the financial accounting and management accounting functions. You work from 9:00am until 5:00pm and are required to have lunch between 12:00pm and 1:00pm.

The following tables show your work schedules for the financial and management accounting functions and detail the days when specific jobs have to be completed and the length of time, in hours, each job takes you to complete. The financial accounting function works on a monthly cycle of work whereas the management accounting function works on a weekly cycle of work. For the financial accounting function, work is required by the end of the day identified in the work schedule.

| | Financial accounting function work schedule | | | | |
	Monday	**Tuesday**	**Wednesday**	**Thursday**	**Friday**
Week 1	Bank reconciliation (2 hours)			Bank monies (2 hours)	Trade receivable review (3 hours)
Week 2		Petty cash top up (2 hours)	Supplier payments (3 hours)	Bank monies (2 hours)	
Week 3	Bank reconciliation (2 hours)	Accruals and prepayments (2 hours)		Bank monies (2 hours)	Trade receivable review (3 hours)
Week 4	Wages analysis (3 hours)		Non-current assets (1 hour)	Bank monies (2 hours)	

Management accounting function work schedule			
Task	Task to be completed by:		Task duration
	Day	Time	
Budget run	Friday	09:00	4 hours
Expenses analysis	Tuesday	14:00	2 hours
Departmental reports	Monday	12:00	2 hours
Inventory review	Friday	10:00	1 hour
Variance report	Every day	14:00	1 hour
Departmental charges	Wednesday	12:00	2 hours

In addition to this information, the whole accounting function has an hour-long meeting at 10:00am on Mondays. Today is Friday in week three of the month.

Complete the to-do list below for next Monday by assigning each task to the correct position.

Please note that each task box is one hour in duration, therefore if a task takes more than one hour to complete you will be able to use the task box more than once.

Monday To-do list	Time
	09:00–10:00
	10:00–11:00
	11:00–12:00
	12:00–13:00
	13:00–14:00
	14:00–15:00
	15:00–16:00
	16:00–17:00

Tasks:

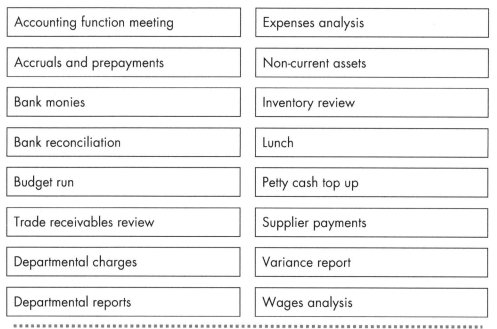

Accounting function meeting	Expenses analysis
Accruals and prepayments	Non-current assets
Bank monies	Inventory review
Bank reconciliation	Lunch
Budget run	Petty cash top up
Trade receivables review	Supplier payments
Departmental charges	Variance report
Departmental reports	Wages analysis

Task 7

A trainee in the accounting function has been asked to take responsibility for learning about the new computerised accounts system that the organisation will start to use in six months' time. The system is being built by an IT developer specifically for the needs of your organisation. After completing personal development activities the trainee will be expected to provide training and support for staff in the accounting function. According to the timescale for this work, all staff will need to start their training on the new system three months prior to the introduction of the new system.

(a) Insert the TWO most appropriate development activities for the trainee to complete, in order to prepare for their work associated with this task, into the boxes provided. You should also identify the timescale for the completion of each of these development activities.

Development activity	Timescale for completion

Development activities and timescales:

Sit with the Finance Director to understand his role	Complete a spreadsheet course at a local college	0–3 months
Complete database training	Attend a one day training course with the developers of the new system	4–6 months
Complete a 'How to provide excellent training' course	Attend an AAT branch meeting	7–12 months
Read AAT magazine	Complete an online word processing course	

(b) **For each of the following statements insert the most appropriate reason into the column to explain why the statement is correct. Note that each reason may only be selected once.**

Statement	Reason
CPD has to be completed by those working in an accounting function because …	
Identifying SMART personal development objectives is important because …	
It is important to discuss personal development with a line manager because …	
An organisation benefits if staff development and CPD activities are completed because …	

Reasons:

they need to know of changes to the organisational structure of their professional body.	it ensures an individual's technical knowledge is up to date.
it looks good to have a large list of CPD activities.	all staff should be SMART.
they may be able to provide a different assessment of your performance and areas for development.	the activities should be clearly identified so that progress and achievement against the objectives can be assessed.
it means that the staff's general standard of work should be improved and should comply with regulatory requirements.	it is good to talk with those who staff report to.

Task 8

(a) Identify which THREE of the following are fundamental ethical principles by writing the appropriate principles in the table:

Principles:

Fundamental ethical principles	Subjectivity	Professionalism
	Good communication	Control
	Objectivity	Honesty
	Happiness	Integration

(b) Write a brief report for finance staff setting out:

1. An introduction to the subject of ethical principles

2. What is meant by professional behaviour

3. Why confidentiality of information must be maintained

4. Why these issues are particularly important in an accounts department

BPP PRACTICE ASSESSMENT 1
LEVEL 2 SYNOPTIC ASSESSMENT

ANSWERS

Level 2 Synoptic Assessment
BPP practice assessment 1

Task 1

(a)

	✓
Production quality control policy	
Website development procedures	
Staff code of behaviour policy	✓
Motor vehicle maintenance policy	

(b)

	✓
Organisations, by law, must have at least ten policies and procedures.	
It is good practice for organisations to have policies and procedures so all staff work to a consistent standard.	✓
Data protection policy is an example of a policy that would not apply to those staff working in an accounting function.	
Organisational procedures always result in staff taking longer to do work tasks.	
Ensuring staff adhere to organisational policies and procedures should result in more efficient working practices.	✓
The Health and Safety policy only applies to those working in the production department.	

(c)

Stakeholders an accounting trainee is most likely to communicate with on a regular basis
HM Revenue & Customs
Trade receivables

(d)

From:	AATstudents@Mbs.com
To:	mslone@mbs.com
Subject:	Meeting room booking

Hello Martin

Paragraph 1

Paragraph 2

Regards

AAT student

	Paragraph 1 ✓	Paragraph 2 ✓
We require a room for our review meeting on 18 August 20XX between 10:00am and 2:00pm. Tea/coffee is not required but lunch is required at 12:00pm. Two people require vegetarian food; the others have no special dietary requirements.		
The room should be arranged in a horseshoe style and an overhead projector, wide screen and laptop will be required for the meeting. The costs associated with the meeting are to be sent for the attention of John Brean. Budget code AC3217653 should be charged.		
The accounting function needs a room for its monthly review meeting on 18 August 20XX. The meeting is due to start at 10:00am and should finish at 2:00pm. There will be 25 people at the meeting and we shall require lunch at 12:00pm; two attendees require vegetarian food, nobody else has any special dietary arrangements. There will not be a requirement for tea or coffee.		

	Paragraph 1 ✓	Paragraph 2 ✓
On behalf of John Brean I write to request a booking for the accounting's function monthly review meeting. There will be 25 staff including the Finance Director and Managing Director attending the meeting and lunch will be required at 12:00pm. The only special dietary requirements are that two people require vegetarian food. Tea/coffee will not be required.		
An overhead projector, white screen and laptop will be required for the meeting. The room should be arranged in our usual style. The costs associated with the meeting are to be sent for the attention of John Brean. Budget code AC3217653 should be charged.		
An overhead projector, white screen and laptop will be required for the meeting. The costs associated with the meeting are to be sent for the attention of John Brean. Budget code ACC3217653 should be charged.		
We will require an overhead projector, white screen and laptop for the meeting. The room should be arranged in our usual horseshoe style. The costs associated with the meeting are to be sent for the attention of John Brean. Budget code ACC3217653 should be charged.		✓
Please arrange for a room to be booked for the accounting function's monthly review meeting. There will be 25 staff plus the Finance Director and Managing Director at the meeting between 10:00am and 2:00pm on 18 August 20XX. Tea/coffee will not be required and lunch is requested at 12:00pm. Two people require vegetarian food; there are no dietary requirements.	✓	

(e) You do not need to proofread emails as this is an informal method of communication. | False |

When deciding upon the best method of communication you only need to consider the information you are trying to communicate. | False |

Task 2

(a)

Statement	True ✓	False ✓
FIFO is a technique used to cost issues and to value inventories	✓	
The piecework method to pay labour guarantees a set amount of wages		✓
A variance calculation measures the difference between revenue and cost		✓
Classification of cost by behaviour allows the planning of total cost at differing levels of output	✓	

(b)

Characteristic	Financial accounting ✓	Management accounting ✓
This system produces statements that are used as a basis to determine the tax charge	✓	
This system uses techniques to cost issues and to value inventories		✓
This system produces statements that are primarily for internal use		✓
This system produces statements that have many external users	✓	

Task 3

(a) Sales ledger

Account name	Amount £	Debit	Credit
Wem Designs	1,128		✓
Bailey and Byng	354		✓

(b) General ledger

Account name	Amount £	Debit	Credit
Sales returns	1,235	✓	
VAT	247	✓	
Sales ledger control	1,482		✓

(c) J B Mills

Date 20XX	Details	Amount £	Date 20XX	Details	Amount £
1 Jun	Balance b/f	1,585	22 Jun	Bank	678
11 Jun	Invoice 1269	1,804	29 Jun	Credit note 049	607
			30 Jun	Balance c/d	2,104
	Total	3,389		Total	3,389
1 Jul	Balance b/d	2,104			

Task 4

(a)

Account name	Amount £	Debit ✓	Credit ✓
Capital	4,780		✓
Office expenses	1,927	✓	
Sales	8,925		✓
Purchases	4,212	✓	
Commission received	75		✓
Discounts received	54		✓
Cash at bank	1,814	✓	
Petty cash	180	✓	
Loan from bank	5,000		✓
Motor expenses	372	✓	
Motor vehicles	9,443	✓	
Other expenses	886	✓	
Journal to record opening entries of new business.			

(b)

From:	Accountingtechnician@ABC.com
To:	Khancatering@info.com
Cc:	Jacksterling@ABC.com
Subject	The purpose of a journal, and the types of entries that can be recorded
Date:	01/08/20XX

Good afternoon Jessica,

My supervisor Jack Sterling has asked me to contact you and answer your query regarding the purpose of a journal, and the types of entries that can be recorded.

A journal can be used to record bookkeeping transactions that may not appear in any other books of prime entry.

The entries in a journal will follow the concept of double-entry, so that journal entries are made using debits and credits to record assets, liabilities, income, expenses and capital balances.

The use of a journal can include:

1. Posting opening balances
2. Writing off irrecoverable debts
3. Recording payroll transactions
4. Correction of errors

I hope that I have answered your query on the use of journal entries.

Please do not hesitate to contact me if I can help in any other way.

Thank you.

Kind regards,

Your name

Accounting Technician

Task 5

(a) **Working:** £21,999 + £1,649 = £23,648

Account name	Amount £	Debit ✓	Credit ✓
Wages expense	23,648	✓	
Wages control	23,648		✓

(b) **Working:** £21,999 – £5,755 – £1,476 – £750

Account name	Amount £	Debit ✓	Credit ✓
Wages control	14,018	✓	
Bank	14,018		✓

Task 6

Monday To-do list	Time
Department reports	09:00–10:00
Accounting function meeting	10:00–11:00
Departmental reports	11:00–12:00
Lunch	12:00–13:00
Variance report	13:00–14:00
Wages analysis	14:00–15:00
Wages analysis	15:00–16:00
Wages analysis	16:00–17:00

Task 7

(a)

Development activity	Timescale for completion
Complete a 'How to provide excellent training' course	0–3 months
Attend one day training course with the developers of the new system	0–3 months

(b)

Statement	Reason
CPD has to be completed by those working in an accounting function because ...	it ensures an individual's technical knowledge is up to date.
Identifying SMART personal development objectives is important because ...	the activities should be clearly identified so that progress and achievement against the objectives can be assessed.
It is important to discuss personal development with a line manager because ...	they may be able to provide a different assessment of your performance and areas for development.
An organisation benefits if staff development and CPD activities are completed because ...	it means that the staff's general standard of work should be improved and should comply with regulatory requirements.

Task 8

(a)

Fundamental ethical principles
Objectivity
Professionalism
Honesty

(b)

Ethics is a set of moral principles that guides personal behaviour and must also guide behaviour in business.

Professional behaviour is one of the fundamental principles in the AAT Code of Ethics. It requires an AAT member to comply with the law and avoid any action that brings the profession into disrepute.

The confidentiality of information acquired as a result of professional and business relationships must be respected. This is an important part of the relationship of trust which must exist with colleagues and clients. You should not use or disclose confidential information unless you are properly authorised to do so or have a legal or professional right or duty to disclose.

An accounts department can be dealing with the financial affairs of a company or the financial affairs of clients. In either situation, accounting staff are trusted to produce accurate financial information and to safeguard the interests of the company or the clients. This requires them to maintain high ethical standards and avoid conflicts of interest.

BPP PRACTICE ASSESSMENT 2
LEVEL 2 SYNOPTIC
ASSESSMENT

Time allowed: 2 hours

Level 2 Synoptic Assessment
BPP practice assessment 2

Task 1

The partially completed organisation chart below shows some of the partners of a chartered accountancy practice and their staff.

(a) Add the correct job titles into the blank spaces to complete the organisation chart.

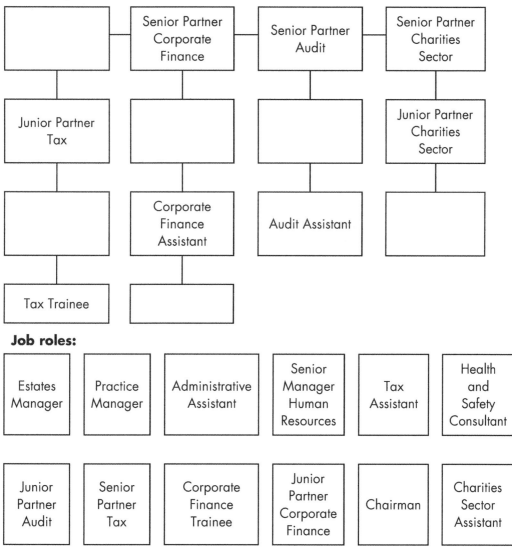

Job roles:

Estates Manager	Practice Manager	Administrative Assistant	Senior Manager Human Resources	Tax Assistant	Health and Safety Consultant
Junior Partner Audit	Senior Partner Tax	Corporate Finance Trainee	Junior Partner Corporate Finance	Chairman	Charities Sector Assistant

(b) **Identify whether the following statements are true or false.**

Statement	True ✓	False ✓
Ensuring the VAT bill is paid on time will help the organisation meet its legal and regulatory requirements.		
Paying supplier invoices as soon as they are received will help the organisation's solvency.		

Task 2

This is a draft of a letter to be addressed to Mrs Oboh, a supplier, to advise her of the results of your reconciliation of the statement of account you received from her. The differences are as follows:

Transaction date	Amount	Comment
12.10.XX	£794.35	The invoice for this entry has been located; however, the invoice total is £749.35.
26.10.XX	£375.29	We have no record of ever ordering or receiving goods to this value from Mrs Oboh.

Review the draft letter and identify EIGHT words or collections of letters or digits which are either spelt incorrectly, are inappropriate or are technically incorrect.

October Statment Reconciliation

Dear Mrs Oboh,

Many thanks for providing the October statement which we have now reviewed and compared to our records of amounts owing by you. We would like too highlight two discrepancies:

1.   Your entry for £794.35 on 12.01.XX does not corespond with the invoice we have for that date. The invoice shows an amount of £749.35 for these goods.

2.   Your entry for £375.29 on 26.10.XX is not known to us. We have no record of ever ordering or sending this amount of goods on this date.

Please investigate these differences as we want to be sure our records agree before we setle our account with you. If you would prefer to contact me by telephone to discuss this matter please do so as we would like to resolve these differences as soon as posible.

Yours sincerely

Task 3

A credit customer, Jae Pih, has ceased trading, owing Gold £2,320 plus VAT.

(a) **Record the journal entries needed in the general ledger to write off the net amount and the VAT.**

Account name	Amount £	Debit ✓	Credit ✓
▼			
▼			
▼			

Picklist:

Gold
Irrecoverable debts
Jae Pih
Purchases
Purchases ledger control
Sales
Sales ledger control
VAT

It is important to understand the types of error that are disclosed by the trial balance and those that are not.

(b) **Show which of the errors below are, or are not, disclosed by the trial balance.**

Errors	Error disclosed by the trial balance ✓	Error NOT disclosed by the trial balance ✓
Recording a bank payment for office expenses on the debit side of the office furniture account.		
Recording a payment for motor expenses in the bank account, the motor expenses account and the miscellaneous expenses account. (Ignore VAT)		

Errors	Error disclosed by the trial balance ✓	Error NOT disclosed by the trial balance ✓
Recording a payment by cheque to a credit supplier in the bank account and purchases ledger control account only.		
Recording a cash payment for travel expenses in the cash account only. (Ignore VAT)		

One of the errors in (b) above can be classified as an error of principle.

(c) **Show which error is an error of principle.**

Errors	✓
Recording a bank payment for office expenses on the debit side of the office furniture account.	
Recording a payment for motor expenses in the bank account, the motor expenses account and the miscellaneous expenses account. (Ignore VAT)	
Recording a payment by cheque to a credit supplier in the bank account and purchases ledger control account only.	
Recording a cash payment for travel expenses in the cash account only. (Ignore VAT)	

Task 4

(a) You are employed by Judson Ltd. Below is a summary of Judson Ltd's account in Gold's purchase ledger. Judson Ltd has agreed to allow Gold to make payments by the last day of the second month following the month of invoice. For example invoices issued in January will be due for payment by 31 March.

Date 20XX	Details	Amount £
1 April	Invoice J338	1,145
3 April	Invoice J345	1,330
7 May	Invoice J401	2,887
7 May	Credit note C025	1,330
26 May	Credit note C033	236
26 May	Invoice J478	7,216
26 June	Invoice J501	442
30 June	Credit note C040	152

Complete the table below by:

- **Inserting the total of transactions with Judson Ltd in each of the months April, May and June.**

- **Showing the dates by which payments should be made by circling the relevant dates.**

Month	Amount £	Payments to be made by
Transactions in April		30 April 31 May 30 June 31 July 31 August
Transactions in May		30 April 31 May 30 June 31 July 31 August
Transactions in June		30 April 31 May 30 June 31 July 31 August

Your manager, Jose Marina, has sent you the memo below which you have received today, 1 November 20XX.

MEMO

As you are aware, we have a special payment arrangement with Gold, an important customer. We have agreed to allow Gold to make payments by the last day of the second month following the month of invoice. The payment terms for other customers are 30 days.

Unfortunately, Gold has been late with payment on the last two scheduled payment dates.

Please prepare a letter, addressed to Gold, explaining when payments should be made, and stating that we may have to reconsider our payment arrangement if future payments are not made by their due date.

Our contact at Gold is Mr Carat, and I would be grateful if you would sign the letter on behalf of our company.

Many thanks

Jose

(b) **Prepare a suitable business letter to Gold, making sure your letter is dated the same date as Jose's memo.**

Judson Ltd

28 Anderson Street, Ainsley, AN21 8EN

Telephone: 01872 890120

Email: **judson@sales.com**

Mr Carat

Gold

14 High Street

Darton, DF11 4GX

Task 5

Gold has received a cheque for £1,512 from a credit customer, B Cohen, in full settlement of the account. There was no document included with the cheque to show what transactions were included in the payment.

(a) Show what document the customer should have included with the cheque by circling one document name.

Document names
Delivery note   Petty cash voucher   Purchase order   Remittance advice note

This is the account of B Cohen in Gold's sales ledger.

B Cohen   **Account code: COH007**

Date 20XX	Details	Amount £	Date 20XX	Details	Amount £
1 Jun	Balance b/f	1,926	3 Jun	Credit note 101	185
25 Jun	Sales invoice 387	314	4 Jun	Bank	1,741
28 Jun	Sales invoice 391	987	21 Jun	Credit note 110	224
29 Jun	Sales invoice 393	1,422			

(b) Using the picklists below, complete the following statement.

The cheque from B Cohen for £1,512 has resulted in an ▼

This probably relates to ▼

In order to resolve the problem Gold should ▼

from B Cohen for £ [   ] which will clear the outstanding balance.

Picklist:

balance b/f
credit note 110
credit note 101
overpayment
request a credit note
request an invoice
request another cheque
sales invoice 387
sales invoice 391
sales invoice 393
underpayment

On 10 July Gold received the following purchase order from B Cohen. The goods were delivered the following day. The customer has been offered an 8% trade discount and a 2.5% prompt payment discount for payment within ten days.

B Cohen
Ravenscourt Road
Darton, DF15 0MX

Purchase Order BCO1157

Gold   10 July 20XX
14 High Street
Darton
DF11 4GX

Please supply 550 units of product code BX26
@ £160.00 per ten, plus VAT.

(c)   Complete the TEN boxes in the sales invoice below.

Gold
14 High Street, Darton, DF11 4GX

SALES INVOICE 427

Date: [▼]

To: B Cohen   Customer account code: [   ]

       Ravenscourt Road
       Darton, DF 15 OMX   Purchase order no: [   ]

Quantity of units	Product code	Price each £	Total amount after trade discount £	VAT £	Total £

Terms: [▼]

Picklist:

10 July 20XX
11 July 20XX
20 July 20XX
21 July 20XX
Net monthly account
30 days net

2.5% prompt payment discount for payment within 10 days
8% trade discount
COH007
BCO1157

....

Task 6

On 28 July, Gold received the following bank statement as at 27 July.

MIDWAY BANK plc				
To: Gold	**52 The Parade, Darton, DF10 9SW** Account No 39103988			27 July 20XX
BANK STATEMENT				
Date 20XX	**Details**	**Paid out £**	**Paid in £**	**Balance £**
01 July	Balance b/f			2,447 D
01 July	Standing order – City Tours	326		
01 July	Cheque 001229	781		
01 July	Direct Debit – ABC Ltd	3,425		
01 July	Counter credit		3,117	3,862 D
12 July	Cheque 001231	1,886		5,748 D
22 July	BACS transfer – Burford Ltd		22,448	
22 July	Cheque 001232	118		16,582 C
27 July	Standing order – Castle and Co	110		
27 July	Bank charges	57		16,415 C
D = Debit C = Credit				

(a)   **Check the items on the bank statement against the items in the cash book.**

(b)   **Enter any items into the cash book as needed.**

(c)   **Total the cash book and clearly show the balance carried down at 27 July and brought down at 28 July.**

Cash book

Date 20XX	Details	Bank £	Date 20XX	Cheque Number	Details	Bank £
01 Jul	Thompson Tubes	3,117	01 Jul		Balance b/f	3,228
20 Jul	Bo Yen	316	01 Jul		City Tours	326
22 Jul	Niche Products	615	01 Jul		ABC Ltd	3,425
27 Jul	Longford Ltd	7,881	02 Jul	001231	Verve Designs	1,886
	▾		08 Jul	001232	Bal Byng	118
	▾		12 Jul	001233	Courtney and Co	4,114
	▾		12 Jul	001234	GHL Ltd	905
	▾		27 Jul		Castle and Co	110
	▾				▾	
	▾				▾	
	Total				Total	
	▾				▾	

Picklist:

ABC Ltd
Bal Byng
Balance b/d
Balance c/d
Bank charges
Bo Yen
Burford Ltd
Castle and Co
Cheque 001229
City Tours
Courtney and Co
GHL Ltd
Longford Ltd
Niche Products
Thompson Tubes
Verve Designs

Task 7

The following table shows budgeted income and variances for last month for Johnson Ltd. It is company policy to provide managers with a variance report highlighting significant variances.

Any variance in excess of 10% is considered significant.

Identify significant variances in excess of 10% of budget, entering S for significant and NS for not significant.

Income/ Expenditure	Budget £	Variance £	Adverse (A) or Favourable (F)	Significant (S) or Not Significant (NS)
Income	45,000	1,500	F	
Material	15,800	3,900	A	
Labour	9,000	890	F	
Overheads	8,800	1,700	A	

Task 8

You have been promoted from Finance Trainee to Assistant Sales Ledger Manager within the finance team of your organisation. A new Finance Trainee is due to start work today; however, the Financial Accountant has been called out of the office for the morning and he has asked you to look after the new Finance Trainee until he returns in the afternoon when he will do the trainee's induction. You have two tasks to finish this morning: a budget analysis for the production department and to check attendance by members of the finance function at a conference.

(a) **From the actions below select the THREE things you will do, during the morning, to help the trainee settle into their new role within your team but also to meet your work commitments to colleagues.**

Action	✓
Tell the Finance Trainee to go home and return after lunch when the Financial Accountant is in the office.	
Meet the Finance Trainee and introduce yourself and explain about the Financial Accountant not being available until lunchtime.	

Action	✓
Contact the production department to advise them of the situation and request an extension to the deadline for the budget analysis information.	
Tell the trainee to sit at a desk and occupy themselves by looking at some leisure magazines whilst you complete your work.	
Ask the trainee to think of what training courses they want to attend.	
Take the trainee with you as you visit members of the department to confirm attendance at the conference, introducing the new team member at the same time.	

(b) **Identify whether the following would or would not necessarily have a positive effect on the team performance of the finance function.**

	Would usually have a positive effect ✓	Would not necessarily have a positive effect ✓
Having a leader who does not encourage communication with other team members		
Ensuring there are at least four members in the team		
Selecting team members that have complementary experiences and skills		

Task 9

Organisations have a moral obligation to implement sustainability initiatives which promote the long-term maintenance and wellbeing of the environment, the economy and society as a whole.

(a) Identify which FOUR of the following are sustainability initiatives that a business may implement.

	✓
Introduce a waste recycling scheme.	
Recruit only fully trained staff.	
Use video conferencing to save staff having to travel to team meetings.	
Increase prices every time costs go up.	
Obtain goods and services from the cheapest supplier.	
Give all staff a pay rise every year.	
Introduce procedures to ensure that all electrical equipment is fully switched off each day when the office is vacated.	
Encourage staff not to print emails unless absolutely necessary.	

(b) Identify whether the following statements are true or false.

Statement	True ✓	False ✓
Sustainability means ensuring the organisation focuses purely on economic growth at all costs.		
Encouraging suppliers to send electronic invoices can be part of an organisation's sustainability agenda.		
When sourcing goods and services an organisation should check that potential suppliers have good environmental policies.		
Planning the routes of delivery vehicles to minimise distance travelled may reduce the running costs of the organisation and also have a positive effect on the environment.		

(c) Write a brief report to finance department staff explaining:

1. **What is meant by CPD**
2. **Why CPD is important for finance staff**
3. **Types of activity which can be undertaken as part of CPD**

BPP PRACTICE ASSESSMENT 2
LEVEL 2 SYNOPTIC ASSESSMENT

ANSWERS

Level 2 Synoptic Assessment
BPP practice assessment 2

Task 1

(a)

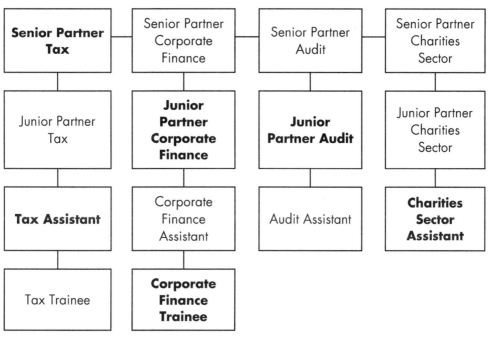

(b)

Statement	True ✓	False ✓
Ensuring the VAT bill is paid on time will help the organisation meet its legal and regulatory requirements.	✓	
Paying supplier invoices as soon as they are received will help the organisation's solvency.		✓

Task 2

October Statement Reconciliation

Dear Mrs Oboh,

Many thanks for providing the October statement which we have now reviewed and compared to our records of amounts owing by you. We would like too highlight two discrepancies:

1. Your entry for £794.35 on 12.01.XX does not correspond with the invoice we have for that date. The invoice shows an amount of £749.35 for these goods.

2. Your entry for £375.29 on 26.10.XX is not known to us. We have no record of ever ordering or sending this amount of goods on this date.

Please investigate these differences as we want to be sure our records agree before we settle our account with you. If you would prefer to contact me by telephone to discuss this matter please do so as we would like to resolve these differences as soon as possible.

Yours sincerely

Task 3

(a)

Account name	Amount £	Debit ✓	Credit ✓
Irrecoverable debts	2,320	✓	
VAT	464	✓	
Sales ledger control	2,784		✓

(b)

Errors	Error disclosed by the trial balance ✓	Error NOT disclosed by the trial balance ✓
Recording a bank payment for office expenses on the debit side of the office furniture account		✓
Recording a payment for motor expenses in the bank account, the motor expenses account and the miscellaneous expenses account. (Ignore VAT)	✓	
Recording a payment by cheque to a credit supplier in the bank account and purchases ledger control account only		✓
Recording a cash payment for travel expenses in the cash account only. (Ignore VAT)	✓	

(c)

Errors	✓
Recording a bank payment for office expenses on the debit side of the office furniture account.	✓
Recording a payment for motor expenses in the bank account, the motor expenses account and the miscellaneous expenses account. (Ignore VAT)	
Recording a payment by cheque to a credit supplier in the bank account and purchases ledger control account only.	
Recording a cash payment for travel expenses in the cash account only. (Ignore VAT)	

Task 4

(a)

Month	Amount £	Payments to be made by
Transactions in April	2,475	30 June
Transactions in May	8,537	31 July
Transactions in June	290	31 August

(b)

Judson Ltd

28 Anderson Street, Ainsley, AN21 8EN

Telephone: 01872 890120

Email: **judson@sales.com**

Mr Carat

Gold

114 High Street

Darton, DF11 4GX

1 November 20XX

Dear Mr Carat,

Late payments

Our records show that your business has been late with its last two scheduled payments to us.

I must remind you that, under the terms of our agreement, payment is expected on the last day of the second month following the month when a sale is invoiced. So, for example, invoices issued by us in November will be due for payment by 31 January.

If you do not pay in accordance with these agreed terms, then we will have to request that all future invoices are settled on our usual terms of business, which is 30 days from the invoice date.

Please let me know if you have any questions regarding our payment terms, or if I can help in any way.

Your sincerely,

Your name
Accounting Technician

Task 5

(a)

Document names
Remittance advice note

(b)

The cheque from B Cohen for £1,512 has resulted in an **underpayment** .

This probably relates to **sales invoice 391** .

In order to resolve the problem Gold should **request another cheque**

from B Cohen for **£ 987** which will clear the outstanding balance.

(c)

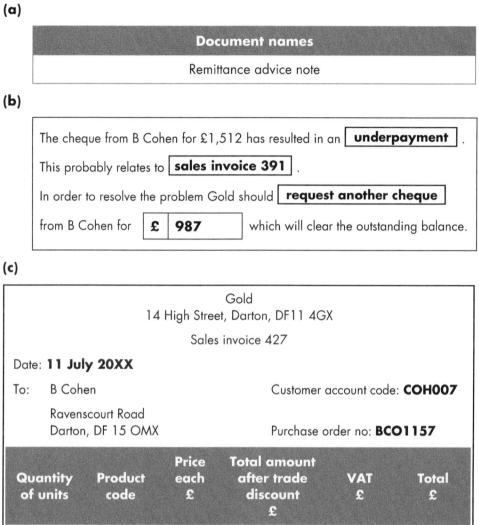

Gold
14 High Street, Darton, DF11 4GX

Sales invoice 427

Date: **11 July 20XX**

To: B Cohen

Customer account code: **COH007**

Ravenscourt Road
Darton, DF 15 OMX

Purchase order no: **BCO1157**

Quantity of units	Product code	Price each £	Total amount after trade discount £	VAT £	Total £
550	BX26	16	8,096.00	1,619.20	9,715.20

Terms: 2.5% prompt payment discount for payment within 10 days

Workings:

$550 \times £16 \times 92\% = £8,096$

$£8,096 \times 0.2 = £1,619.20$

Task 6

Tutorial note. Cheque 001229 for £781 on the bank statement was taken into account in the previous bank reconciliation, since the difference between the opening balance on the bank statement and the cash book is £3,228 – £2,447 = £781. Therefore it should not be entered again into the cash book.

Cash book

Date 20XX	Details	Bank £	Date 20XX	Cheque Number	Details	Bank £
01 Jul	Thompson Tubes	3,117	01 Jul		Balance b/f	3,228
20 Jul	Bo Yen	316	01 Jul		City Tours	326
22 Jul	Niche Products	615	01 Jul		ABC Ltd	3,425
27 Jul	Longford Ltd	7,881	02 Jul	001231	Verve Designs	1,886
22 Jul	Burford Ltd	22,448	08 Jul	001232	Bal Byng	118
			12 Jul	001233	Courtney and Co	4,114
			12 Jul	001234	GHL Ltd	905
			27 Jul		Castle and Co	110
			27 Jul		Bank charges	57
			27 Jul		Balance c/d	20,208
	Total	34,377			Total	34,377
28 Jul	Balance c/d	20,208				

Task 7

Income/ Expenditure	Budget £	Variance £	Adverse (A) or Favourable (F)	Significant (S) or Not Significant (NS)
Income	45,000	1,500	F	NS
Material	15,800	3,900	A	S
Labour	9,000	890	F	NS
Overheads	8,800	1,700	A	S

Task 8

(a)

Action	✓
Tell the Finance Trainee to go home and return after lunch when the Financial Accountant is in the office.	
Meet the Finance Trainee and introduce yourself and explain about the Financial Accountant not being available until lunchtime.	✓
Contact the production department to advise them of the situation and request an extension to the deadline for the budget analysis information.	✓
Tell the trainee to sit at a desk and occupy themselves by looking at some leisure magazines whilst you complete your work.	
Ask the trainee to think of what training courses they want to attend.	
Take the trainee with you as you visit members of the department to confirm attendance at the conference, introducing the new team member at the same time.	✓

(b)

	Would usually have a positive effect ✓	Would not necessarily have a positive effect ✓
Having a leader who does not encourage communication with other team members		✓
Ensuring there are at least four members in the team		✓
Selecting team members that have complementary experiences and skills	✓	

Task 9

(a)

	✓
Introduce a waste recycling scheme.	✓
Recruit only fully trained staff.	
Use video conferencing to save staff having to travel to team meetings.	✓
Increase prices every time costs go up.	
Obtain goods and services from the cheapest supplier.	
Give all staff a pay rise every year.	
Introduce procedures to ensure that all electrical equipment is fully switched off each day when the office is vacated.	✓
Encourage staff not to print emails unless absolutely necessary.	✓

(b)

Statement	True ✓	False ✓
Sustainability means ensuring the organisation focuses purely on economic growth at all costs.		✓
Encouraging suppliers to send electronic invoices can be part of an organisation's sustainability agenda.	✓	
When sourcing goods and services an organisation should check that potential suppliers have good environmental policies.	✓	
Planning the routes of delivery vehicles to minimise distance travelled may reduce the running costs of the organisation and also have a positive effect on the environment.	✓	

(c)

CPD is a process of planning for the future and gaining experience and training which is relevant to the current job role and to future career progression.

Finance staff should undertake CPD in relation to their current position, because their job requires their knowledge and training to be up-to-date. Continued membership of bodies such as AAT requires a certain amount of CPD each year. CPD will also assist finance staff in moving up to higher level jobs.

Skills and knowledge can be developed by attending training courses and seminars. These could be run in-house or by external providers. Technical briefings and updates are also provided by professional bodies such as AAT. There is also on-the-job training, and skills and knowledge that can be learned from more experienced people.

BPP PRACTICE ASSESSMENT 3
LEVEL 2 SYNOPTIC ASSESSMENT

Time allowed: 2 hours

Level 2 Synoptic Assessment
BPP practice assessment 3

Task 1

(a) It is Friday morning. A colleague usually banks the weekly cash on a Friday morning. As the colleague is on holiday, she has left a note asking you to do it. Your line manager has also asked you to complete some project work which you think will take all of Friday. You are not sure that you will have time to do both tasks and you know that the business is suffering from cash flow problems.

Which TWO of the following are possible consequences of you NOT banking the money on Friday?

	✓
The business may have insufficient funds available to pay a debt becoming payable next week	
You will not be able to complete the work for your line manager	
You will be able to complete the work for your line manager	
The money will not have to be banked by someone else	

(b) **Complete the following sentence.**

The most appropriate action to take is:

▼

Picklist:

Bank the money and then move on to the project work
Complete the project work and bank the money next week
Explain the situation to your manager and try to find a solution
Throw away the note from your colleague and claim you did not receive it

Your weekly workload (excluding completed tasks) is shown in the table below. You need to carry out all these tasks, but you also have to respond to business needs as required. Your working day is 9:30am to 5:30pm. Your lunch break is an hour long (12:30pm to 1:30pm). It is 9:30am on Wednesday and you have completed your routine tasks on time so far this week.

Your remaining tasks for the week are as follows:

| Task | Task to be completed by: | | Task duration |
	Day	Time	
Receivables reconciliation	Thursday	09:30	45 minutes
Supplier statement reconciliations	Thursday	10:15	1 hour
Calculate depreciation and process the related journals	Wednesday	11:30	1.5 hours
Collect and distribute post	Every day	10:00	30 minutes
Enter cash payments and receipts	Every day	17:00	3 hours
Prepare payroll listing	Friday	15:00	1 hour
Bank reconciliation	Friday	13:00	2 hours

On arriving at your desk, you pick up an email informing you that the Managing Director has called a meeting to brief all employees on a proposed project to relocate the business to another nearby premises. All employees must attend the briefing at 11:30am which will last for 1 hour.

(c) **Complete the to-do list below for Wednesday by selecting the appropriate tasks from the picklist provided.**

Wednesday To-do list	Order of task completion
▼	First task
▼	Second task
▼	Third task
▼	Fourth task
▼	Fifth task
▼	Sixth task

Picklist:

Bank reconciliation
Briefing from Managing Director
Calculate depreciation and process the related journals
Collect and distribute post
Enter cash payments and receipts
Prepare payroll listing
Receivables reconciliation
Supplier statement reconciliations

(d) **This is a draft of a letter to be addressed to Mrs Baxter, a supplier, querying an invoice because the goods she supplied were damaged when they arrived.**

Review the draft letter and identify FIVE words which are spelled incorrectly, or are inappropriate. **(6 marks)**

Hello Ms Baxter

I am writing to query an invoice with reference AB123. The invoice is for goods we received from you on 1 July 20XX. A copy of invoice AB123 is inclosed.

Staff at our warehouse inspected the goods when they arrived and found that they had been damaged in transit. In accordance with the contract we have in place with you, the goods are being returned to you and I would be greatful if you could issue a credit note for the full amount shown on invoice AB123.

We look forward to hearing from you.

Yours hopefully

Task 2

Gold's trial balance was extracted and did not balance. The debit column of the trial balance totalled £395,222 and the credit column totalled £395,141.

(a) **What entry would be needed in the suspense account to balance the trial balance?**

Account name	Amount £	Debit ✓	Credit ✓
Suspense			

The error in the trial balance has now been identified as arising from an incorrectly totalled VAT column in the cash book, as shown below.

Cash book

Date 20XX	Details	Bank £	Date 20XX	Details	Bank £	VAT £	Trade payables £	Cash purchases £
30 Jun	Balance b/f	14,197	30 Jun	James Jones	654	109		545
30 Jun	Baker and Co	1,445	30 Jun	BDL Ltd	6,197		6,197	
			30 Jun	Connor Smith	474	79		395
			30 Jun	Balance c/d	8,317			
	Total	15,642		Totals	15,642	269	6,197	940

(b) Record the journal entry needed in the general ledger to remove the incorrect entry that was made from the cash book.

Account name	Amount £	Debit ✓	Credit ✓
▼			

(c) Record the journal entry needed in the general ledger to record the correct entry that should have been made from the cash book.

Account name	Amount £	Debit ✓	Credit ✓
▼			

(d) Record the journal entry needed in the general ledger to remove the suspense account balance arising from the error in the cash book.

Account name	Amount £	Debit ✓	Credit ✓
▼			

Picklist:
Balance b/f
Balance c/d
Bank
Cash purchases
Suspense
Total
Trade payables
VAT

The journal is a book of prime entry.

(e)   Show ONE reason for maintaining the journal.

	✓
To detect fraud	
To record goods bought on credit	
To record goods sold on credit	
To record non-regular transactions	

Task 3

(a) **Identify the type of cost behaviour (fixed, variable or semi-variable) described in each statement by putting a tick in the relevant column of the table below.**

Statement	Fixed ✓	Variable ✓	Semi-variable ✓
Costs of £2 per unit at 20,000 units and £10 per unit at 4,000 units			
Costs of £30,000 are made up of a fixed charge of £10,000 and a further cost of £5 per unit at 4,000 units			
Costs are £25,000 units at 10,000 units and £40,000 at 16,000 units			

(b) **Classify the following costs as either fixed or variable by putting a tick in the relevant column of the table below.**

Costs	Fixed ✓	Variable ✓
Materials used in the production of a product		
Employees paid on a time-rate basis for an agreed number of hours per week		
Annual Health and Safety inspection		

Westley Ltd makes a single product and has the following income and expenditure data:

Sales Revenue	£8 per unit
Variable Costs	£5 per unit
Fixed Costs	£10,000 per month

The number of units sold by Westley during the last three months is as follows:

January	2,000 units
February	4,000 units
March	5,000 units

The table below has been partly completed in order to provide income and expenditure information for the three months.

(c) **Complete the formatting of the table by selecting column headings from the picklist. Complete the table by inserting the figures for February, March and Total.**

	▼	Fixed Cost £	▼	Sales Revenue £	▼
January	10,000	10,000	20,000	16,000	(4,000)
February					
March					
Total					

Picklist:

Fixed Costs £
Profit/(Loss) £
Sales Revenue £
Total Costs £
Variable Costs £

Task 4

Purchase invoices and purchase credit notes have been received and partially entered in the day books, as shown below.

Complete the entries in the purchases day book and the purchases returns day book by:

(a) **Selecting the correct supplier account codes from the coding list below.**

(b) **Inserting the appropriate figures to complete the entries.**

Coding list

Supplier name	Supplier account code
Cox and Co	COX001
GBL Ltd	GBL001
R King	KIN001
JAB Ltd	JAB001
Jackson plc	JAC002
Johnson Ltd	JOH003
PDL Designs	PDL001
K Ponti	PON002
Proctor Ltd	PRO003

Purchases day book

Date 20XX	Details	Supplier account code	Invoice number	Total £	VAT £	Net £	Product A100 £	Product B100 £
30 Jun	GBL Ltd	▼	G1161	348		290		290
30 Jun	Jackson plc	▼	4041		125		625	
30 Jun	R King	▼	J1126	612			275	235

Picklist:

COX001
GBL001
KIN001
JAB001
JAC002
JOH003
PDL001
PON002
PRO003

Purchases returns day book

Date 20XX	Details	Supplier account code	Credit note number	Total £	VAT £	Net £	Product A100 £	Product B100 £
30 Jun	PDL Designs	▼	CN110				560	200
30 Jun	K Ponti	▼	398C		95		225	250

Picklist:

COX001
GBL001
KIN001
JAB001
JAC002
JOH003
PDL001
PON002
PRO003

Jason is a new member of staff, and during his induction he asked you the purpose of having a coding system for customers and suppliers.

It is the morning of 1 October and you are drafting an email in response to Jason.

(c)   Complete the email below to answer Jason's query regarding coding systems for customers and suppliers.

From:	Accountingtechnician@XYZ.com
To:	Jason@XYZ.com
Cc:	
Subject:	Purpose of coding systems
Date:	01/10/20XX

Task 5

There are many benefits of employees undergoing Continuing Professional Development (CPD). The ongoing development of relevant skills and knowledge can be beneficial to both the individual and the organisation.

(a) **Indicate whether the following statements in relation to CPD, training and development are true or false.**

Statement	True/False
Employers who invest in the ongoing training and development of employees will need to increase supervision of those employees in the long term.	▼
Employers are solely responsible for ensuring employees meet their CPD requirements.	▼
CPD requirements usually only apply to full members rather than student members of professional accountancy bodies.	▼
Although accountancy bodies require their members to undertake CPD, members are not required to keep a record of their CPD activity.	▼

Picklist:

True
False

You work as an accounts assistant reporting to the accounting department manager. No staff report to you.

A recent appraisal with your manager highlighted that despite your many strengths (including being proficient in the use of spreadsheets and computerised accounting packages) you have two weaknesses that have become apparent over the last six months. These are preventing you from completing your tasks as efficiently as you could do.

The weaknesses are:

• You are too willing to take on extra work when you already have a full workload.

• Your word processing skills are poor and this means it takes you a long time to complete routine correspondence.

(b) Indicate which TWO of the following development opportunities could address these weaknesses.

	✓
Attend a leadership course aimed at improving management skills.	
Attend a training course aimed at improving assertiveness.	
Study the quickstart guide that accompanies the computerised accounting package you use.	
Complete an online course which takes you through the key features of word processing packages and how to use them.	
Complete an online course which takes you through the key features of spreadsheet packages and how to use them.	

Task 6

(a) Identify which THREE of the following are fundamental ethical principles by writing (CBT: drag and drop) the appropriate principles into the table:

Fundamental ethical principles

Picklist:

Confidentiality
Control
Due care
Materiality
Peace of mind
Professional competence

(b) **State which ONE of the following situations is an example of where a conflict of interest may arise:**

	✓
You regularly complete accounting work at a client's premises.	
Your manager takes the whole department for a meal at lunchtime to celebrate the year's financial results.	
You are asked to audit the accounts of your aunt's business when you have been writing up the books for the past year.	
You are asked to complete the accounts of a local car retailer from which your family often purchase their cars.	

(c) **Identify whether the following statements are true or false:**

Statement	True ✓	False ✓
Those working within an accounting environment do not need to act with integrity.		
Personal information of a client cannot be given to other people unless the client authorises it.		
Information about the income generated by a client listed on the stock exchange can be discussed with your friends as at the end of the year the organisation will publish its financial results.		
A conflict of interest never has to be declared if the employee feels happy about the situation.		

(d) **Identify which THREE of the following are sustainability initiatives which a business may implement:**

	✓
Hold all meetings face to face rather than virtually.	
Have all corridor, hall, and passage lighting linked to motion sensors so they automatically switch off when no one is using them.	
Always select the most competitively priced suppliers of goods and services.	
Ensure all qualified accountants complete CPD.	
Do business with any organisations regardless of their environmental practices.	
Ensure costs and expenses are minimised in every instance.	
Arrange monthly management meetings virtually rather than at head office.	
Encourage employees not to print out emails.	

(e) **Write a short report for non-finance staff explaining:**

1. **What is meant by corporate social responsibility (CSR)**

2. **What is meant by the 'triple bottom line' approach**

3. **Some examples of good practice in CSR for an organisation**

Task 7

Gold maintains a petty cash book as a book of prime entry and part of the double entry bookkeeping system.

This is a summary of petty cash transactions in a week:

Train fare paid of £37.05, VAT not applicable.

Envelopes purchased for £20.50, plus VAT at 20%.

(a) **Enter the above transactions into the partially completed petty cash book below.**

(b) **Total the petty cash book and show the balance carried down.**

Petty cash book

Details	Amount £	Details	Amount £	VAT £	Travel expenses £	Office expenses £
Balance b/d	120.00	Pens	30.00			30.00
		▼				
		▼				
		▼				
Total	120.00	Totals				

Picklist:

Balance b/d
Balance c/d
Envelopes
Office expenses
Train fare
Travel expenses
VAT

BPP PRACTICE ASSESSMENT 3
LEVEL 2 SYNOPTIC ASSESSMENT

ANSWERS

Level 2 Synoptic Assessment
BPP practice assessment 3

Task 1

(a)

	✓
The business may have insufficient funds available to pay a debt becoming payable next week	✓
You will not be able to complete the work for your line manager	
You will be able to complete the work for your line manager	✓
The money will not have to be banked by someone else	

(b)

Explain the situation to your manager and try to find a solution

(c)

Wednesday To-do list	Order of task completion
Collect and distribute post	First task
Calculate depreciation and process the related journals	Second task
Briefing from Managing Director	Third task
Enter cash payments and receipts	Fourth task
Receivables reconciliation	Fifth task
Supplier statement reconciliations	Sixth task

This results in the following timetable and ensures all tasks are completed on time:

Task/break	Duration (hrs)	Task order	Time period
Collect and distribute post	0.5	First task	09:30 to 10:00
Calculate depreciation and process the related journals	1.5	Second task	10:00 to 11:30
Briefing from Managing Director	1	Third task	11:30 to 12:30
LUNCH	1		12:30 to 13:30
Enter cash payments and receipts	3	Fourth task	13:30 to 16:30
Receivables reconciliation	0.75	Fifth task	16:30 to 17:15
Supplier statement reconciliations	0.25 (of 1)	Sixth task	17:15 to 17:30*

*Starting this task will mean it can be completed before the deadline on Thursday since there will only be 45 more minutes' worth of work to do on Thursday morning.

(d) The incorrect/inappropriate words are underlined and in bold.

Hello Ms Baxter

I am writing to query an invoice with reference AB123. The invoice is for goods we received from you on 1 July 20XX. A copy of invoice AB123 is **inclosed**.

Staff at our warehouse inspected the goods when they arrived and found that they had been damaged in transit. In accordance with the contract we have in place with you, the goods are being returned to you and I would be **greatful** if you could issue a credit note for the full amount shown on invoice AB123.

We look forward to hearing from you.

Yours **hopefully**

Tutorial note. The corrected letter would look like this:

Dear Mrs Baxter

I am writing to query an invoice with reference AB123. The invoice is for goods we received from you on 1 July 20XX. A copy of invoice AB123 is **enclosed**.

Staff at our warehouse inspected the goods when they arrived and found that they had been damaged in transit. In accordance with the contract we have in place with you, the goods are being returned to you and I would be **grateful** if you could issue a credit note for the full amount shown on invoice AB123.

We look forward to hearing from you.

Yours **sincerely**

Task 2

(a)

Account name	Amount £	Debit ✓	Credit ✓
Suspense	81		✓

The error in the trial balance has now been identified as arising from an incorrectly totalled VAT column in the cash book, as shown below.

Cash book

Date 20XX	Details	Bank £	Date 20XX	Details	Bank £	VAT £	Trade payables £	Cash purchases £
30 Jun	Balance b/f	14,197	30 Jun	James Jones	654	109		545
30 Jun	Baker and Co	1,445	30 Jun	BDL Ltd	6,197		6,197	
			30 Jun	Connor Smith	474	79		395
			30 Jun	Balance c/d	8,317			
	Total	15,642		Totals	15,642	269	6,197	940

(b)

Account name	Amount £	Debit ✓	Credit ✓
VAT	269		✓

(c)

Account name	Amount £	Debit ✓	Credit ✓
VAT	188	✓	

(d)

Account name	Amount £	Debit ✓	Credit ✓
Suspense	81	✓	

(e)

	✓
To detect fraud	
To record goods bought on credit	
To record goods sold on credit	
To record non-regular transactions	✓

Task 3

(a)

Statement	Fixed ✓	Variable ✓	Semi-variable ✓
Costs of £2 per unit at 20,000 units and £10 per unit at 4,000 units (W1)	✓		
Costs of £30,000 are made up of a fixed charge of £10,000 and a further cost of £5 per unit at 4,000 units			✓
Costs are £25,000 units at 10,000 units and £40,000 at 16,000 units (W2)		✓	

Workings:

1. 20,000 × £2 = £40,000; 4,000 × £10 = £40,000. Therefore this is a fixed cost

2. £25,000/10,000 = £2.50 per unit; £40,000/16,000 = £2.50 per unit. Therefore this is a variable cost

(b)

Costs	Fixed ✓	Variable ✓
Materials used in the production of a product		✓
Employees paid on a time-rate basis for an agreed number of hours per week	✓	
Annual Health and Safety inspection	✓	

(c)

	Variable Costs £	Fixed Cost £	Total Costs £	Sales Revenue £	Profit/ (Loss) £
January	10,000	10,000	20,000	16,000	(4,000)
February	20,000	10,000	30,000	32,000	2,000
March	25,000	10,000	35,000	40,000	5,000
Total	55,000	30,000	85,000	88,000	3,000

Task 4

(a)–(b)

Purchases day book

Date 20XX	Details	Supplier account code	Invoice number	Total £	VAT £	Net £	Product A100 £	Product B100 £
30 Jun	GBL Ltd	GBL001	G1161	348	58	290		290
30 Jun	Jackson plc	JAC002	4041	750	125	625	625	
30 Jun	R King	KIN001	J1126	612	102	510	275	235

Purchases returns day book

Date 20XX	Details	Supplier account code	Credit note number	Total £	VAT £	Net £	Product A100 £	Product B100 £
30 Jun	PDL Designs	PDL001	CN110	912	152	760	560	200
30 Jun	K Ponti	PON002	398C	570	95	475	225	250

(c)

From:	Accountingtechnician@XYZ.com
To:	Jason@XYZ.com
Cc:	
Subject:	Purpose of coding systems
Date:	01/10/20XX

Good morning Jason,

Thank you for attending your induction, and I hope you are settling well into your new role.

You may recall at your induction you asked about the purpose of having a coding system for customers and suppliers.

The purpose of having a coding system is to ensure that information, for example invoices and credit notes, are recorded in our accounting system accurately.

Having a unique code for each customer and supplier makes it easy to identify each one, and this helps when communicating with them, as well as with the preparation of management reports.

Coding systems also assist with the filing of information. For example, if a customer has a query on their account we can quickly retrieve any supporting documentation using their unique customer code.

I hope that I have answered your query on the purpose of coding systems, but please let me know if I can clarify anything.

Regards,

Your name
Accounting Technician

Task 5

(a)

Statement	True/False
Employers who invest in the ongoing training and development of employees will need to increase supervision of those employees in the long term.	False
Employers are solely responsible for ensuring employees meet their CPD requirements.	False
CPD requirements usually only apply to full members rather than student members of professional accountancy bodies.	False
Although accountancy bodies require their members to undertake CPD, members are not required to keep a record of their CPD activity.	False

Reasoning:

Employers who invest in the ongoing training and development of employees should be able to **decrease** supervision of those employees in the long term as they become more skilled.

Employees are responsible for their CPD and should work with their employee to undertake suitable learning and development.

CPD requirements **apply to both full members and student members** of professional accountancy bodies.

CPD activity should be recorded.

(b)

	✓
Attend a leadership course aimed at improving management skills.	
Attend a training course aimed at improving assertiveness.	✓
Study the quickstart guide that accompanies the computerised accounting package you use.	
Complete an online course which takes you through the key features of word processing packages and how to use them.	✓
Complete an online course which takes you through the key features of spreadsheet packages and how to use them.	

Task 6

(a)

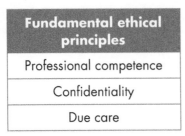

Fundamental ethical principles
Professional competence
Confidentiality
Due care

(b)

	✓
You regularly complete accounting work at a client's premises.	
Your manager takes the whole department for a meal at lunchtime to celebrate the year's financial results.	
You are asked to audit the accounts of your aunt's business when you have been writing up the books for the past year.	✓
You are asked to complete the accounts of a local car retailer from which your family often purchase their cars.	

(c)

Statement	True ✓	False ✓
Those working within an accounting environment do not need to act with integrity.		✓
Personal information of a client cannot be given to other people unless the client authorises it.	✓	
Information about the income generated by a client listed on the stock exchange can be discussed with your friends as at the end of the year the organisation will publish its financial results.		✓
A conflict of interest never has to be declared if the employee feels happy about the situation.		✓

(d)

	✓
Hold all meetings face to face rather than virtually.	
Have all corridor, hall, and passage lighting linked to motion sensors so they automatically switch off when no one is using them.	✓
Always select the most competitively priced suppliers of goods and services.	
Ensure all qualified accountants complete CPD.	
Do business with any organisations regardless of their environmental practices.	
Ensure costs and expenses are minimised in every instance.	
Arrange monthly management meetings virtually rather than at head office.	✓
Encourage employees not to print out emails.	✓

(e)

CSR is a business practice that involves participating in initiatives that benefit society. As consumers become more aware about global social issues, they look at an organisation's CSR when deciding where to spend their money. CSR is now also increasingly a factor in where talented people choose to work.

According to the 'triple bottom line' approach, a company should report three bottom lines. One is the traditional measure of 'profit after tax'. The second is the bottom line of the organisation's 'people account' – how socially responsible its operations have been. The third is the bottom line of its 'planet account' – a measure of how environmentally responsible it has been. A TBL report takes full account of all the costs of being in business.

A primary focus of CSR is the environment. Business should seek to reduce their carbon footprint and consider issues of pollution and depletion of the earth's resources. Many organisations donate time or money to charities as part of their CSR. CSR also demands ethical labour practices, particularly in relation to employees in overseas locations.

Task 7

(a)–(b)

Petty cash-book

Tutorial note. The pens would have been subject to VAT if the seller had been VAT-registered, but clearly this was not the case here, and you were not asked to analyse them anyway.

Details	Amount £	Details	Amount £	VAT £	Travel expenses £	Office expenses £
Balance b/f	120.00	Pens	30.00			30.00
		Train fare	37.05		37.05	
		Envelopes	24.60	4.10		20.50
		Balance c/d	28.35			
Total	120.00	Totals	120.00	4.10	37.05	50.50